THE LOST ART OF CLOSING

The
LOST ART
of CLOSING

Winning the Ten Commitments That Drive Sales

ANTHONY IANNARINO

PORTFOLIO/PENGUIN

Portfolio/Penguin
An imprint of Penguin Random House LLC
375 Hudson Street
New York, New York 10014
penguin.com

Most Portfolio books are available at a discount when purchased in quantity for sales promotions or corporate use. Special editions, which include personalized covers, excerpts, and corporate imprints, can be created when purchased in large quantities. For more information, please call (212) 572-2232 or e-mail specialmarkets@penguinrandomhouse.com. Your local bookstore can also assist with discounted bulk purchases using the Penguin Random House corporate Business-to-Business program. For assistance in locating a participating retailer, e-mail B2B@penguinrandomhouse.com.

Foreword by Brent Adamson and Nicholas Toman. Copyright © 2017 Gartner Inc. and/or its affiliates. All Rights Reserved.

9780735211698 (hardcover)
9780735211704 (e-book)

Printed in the United States of America
10 9 8 7 6 5 4 3 2 1

Book design by Daniel Lagin

For the agitators, instigators, catalysts, and change agents.
You make the world a better place.

CONTENTS

CONTENTS

FOREWORD

OF ALL THE OBSERVATIONS WE MAKE IN *THE CHALLENGER Customer*, perhaps the most foundational is the dramatically increasing complexity of a typical B2B purchase. While B2B sales professionals often lament about the rapidly rising complexity of selling solutions, the far tougher challenge today isn't selling them, but *buying* them.

For many, it's a surprising conclusion. If anything, today's customers seem far more empowered than ever before. With easy access to information, they can now independently identify *more* options across *more* suppliers—all without meeting a single sales rep or taking an actual sales call. Meanwhile, supported by *more* colleagues across *more* parts of their organization, customers come to the table *more* determined and better equipped to extract *more* value across *more* suppliers' capabilities, all at *less* cost. In fact, we often refer to this new reality simply as the "World of More." If you're selling in the World of More, it's hard to imagine that customers need any additional help buying when they're doing such a good job putting pressure on suppliers already.

But if we take off our selling hats for a moment and place ourselves in our customers' shoes, we find the world of buying doesn't feel much better. In all of our recent research into B2B buying, we've found the same theme again and again. Somewhere across the last several years, we've hit a tipping point where customers are empowered with more information and more options, but more customers have become rapidly overwhelmed with *too much* information, *too many* options, and *too many* people. For example, we've found the average B2B solutions purchase typically requires input from at least 6.8 individual customer stakeholders. As all of those different people collect and consider an increasingly vast array of easily accessible information spanning an ever-expanding range of possible options, more often than not the purchase process simply grinds to a halt. Customers fall into endless learning loops, where each piece of additional information raises new questions requiring still more research. The consideration of a wide set of options leads to what author Barry Schwartz refers to as the "paradox of choice," hampering customers' ability to choose one option over another. And ever-larger buying groups representing diverse organizational priorities struggle to find common ground on next steps, let alone an ultimate purchase decision.

The end result? Frustration. Exhaustion. Resignation. And time. In fact, a whole lot of time. In our most recent research, 65 percent of customers told us that the amount of time it took just to get to the point where they were ready to contact a supplier in the first place took as much time as they had originally budgeted for the entire purchase. In other words, it's not sales reps' inability to sell that slows things down, but customers' own struggles to buy. Yet both suppliers *and* customers equally pay the price as commerce in this world comes grinding to a slow crawl.

It's really no wonder that most B2B suppliers tell us their number one competitor today isn't so much the competition as it is the status quo. Therein lies a hugely important lesson for all sales professionals. The shortest path to improved sales success lies in what Anthony

Iannarino refers to as a "customer-oriented" approach to sales. Specifically, working with customers to identify predictable purchase obstacles, and then ensuring both their ability and commitment to moving forward at each purchase stage.

This is the new "close" in sales. Not closing customers on a *sale*, but "closing" customers on each of a series of necessary steps designed to prevent a *purchase stall*. As Anthony puts it, "closing isn't a single event, but a whole series of events. . . . And successfully navigating each one is vital for movement to the next."

How does one win customer commitment at each of those vital moments? That's what *The Lost Art of Closing* is all about. Though in many ways that art isn't really lost at all. It's actually a new art altogether—winning customer commitment at ten specific moments along the purchase journey, specifically designed to "close" that part of the purchase and purposefully move customers on to the next.

With all kinds of practical help targeted to the far more pressing challenge of solution selling today, Anthony has created an invaluable step-by-step guide sure to improve the chances of any sales professional to win more business. We think it's a fantastic read, and we're sure you will too.

Brent Adamson and Nicholas Toman
Coauthors of *The Challenger Customer*

PROLOGUE

A Sort of Apology to the Reader

IF YOU READ MY PREVIOUS BOOK, RIGHT NOW YOU ARE SAYING to yourself, "I thought you told me that *The Only Sales Guide You'll Ever Need* was the only sales guide I would ever need."

You didn't really expect that I wouldn't write another book, did you?

TOSG is a pretty comprehensive guide to selling, now isn't it? You'll no doubt do well by doing the work in that book. But selling is a complex, dynamic human interaction, and there's a greater level of performance available to you if you want it.

The truth is, I had to write this book.

The very idea of closing has changed so much that nothing that has been written before takes the new realities of sales and selling into account. The very word "closing" signifies only one of the many commitments you need to gain to create and win new opportunities. Right now, a lot of people are giving salespeople the advice that they should "never be closing," when in fact you now need to gain at least ten commitments throughout your sales process, and maybe even more.

Historically, books on closing have started with a premise that the final ask was the most difficult part of selling. Those books started with the premise that you needed all kinds of fancy tricks and tactics to close a deal. Now that final commitment is one of the easier commitments to gain. It's all the commitments leading up to the final "ask" that cause us trouble.

There are too many good salespeople struggling to produce the results they need. There are too many sales organizations with pipelines full of so-called opportunities that are stalled, stuck, or something less than an opportunity. Worse still, there is still so much bad advice being doled out by charlatans and nonpracticing theorists that it is no longer possible for me to sit idly by and do nothing.

You'll have to forgive me for writing another sales guide that you absolutely need. You can thank me after you read and put this book to use.

This is a closing book for B2B sales professionals for whom the old closing books won't be of any benefit. This is a modern salesperson's *Secrets of Closing the Sale* by Zig Ziglar or *The Art of Closing the Sale: The Key to Making More Money Faster in the World of Professional Selling* by Brian Tracy.

If this works for you, and there is nothing else you need, can we go ahead and begin working on improving your ability to close deals?

THE LOST ART OF CLOSING

INTRODUCTION

I WAS REHEARSING AND PLAYING SOME SHOWS WITH MY YOUNG rock-and-roll band, Bad Reputation, and, at twenty-one, had finally saved the money to buy a nice PA system. Needing some way to transport my new equipment, I drove to the largest car dealership in Columbus, Ohio, looking for a minivan I could use to haul my gear.

Upon pulling into the car lot, I was immediately approached by a salesperson. He wasn't too aggressive and seemed helpful. He asked me what I was looking for and how much I wanted my car payment to be, and I told him what I was willing to pay monthly. He then escorted me to a massive line of automobiles that might meet my needs. After looking at a number of choices, I selected one that seemed big enough for my gear at a price I could easily afford. I'd driven all kinds of beaters as a kid, so this would be the eighteenth or nineteenth car I owned, but only the second one I'd bought new. (I started with a '67 Mustang, then a '71 Barracuda, a '68 Thunderbird, a terrible old Corvair, a seventy-something Nova, an old Opal, a beat-up Camaro, an '83 Trans Am, and many more I can no longer remember. When all you can afford is a cheap old car, you tend to run through them pretty fast.)

The salesperson started working on the paperwork and then said,

"We can get you very close to where you need to be." He showed me a worksheet with a payment just slightly higher than I'd mentioned earlier. No other numbers, just the monthly payment. Believing that I had to negotiate, I told him he had to do better.

The salesman went to speak to his manager, and they both returned. The sales manager said, "If I can get you to the exact monthly payment you want, will you sign here committing to buy?" I said, "Yes, but let me do some math."

I multiplied the payment by four years.

"So the total amount you're charging me for the car is the monthly payment times forty-eight months, plus interest, right?"

The sales manager corrected me. "No. It's seventy-two months."

Shocked, I replied, "There is no way I would buy a car over six years. I'll be twenty-eight years old when I pay it off!" The sales manager was unmoved. "Look, everybody is buying cars this way now. The seventy-two months is what allows us to give you the low payment you need."

I knew he was trying to take advantage of me.

"I'll pass," I said, grabbing my keys and starting for the door.

The sales manager stood up, blocked the door, and said, "I can't let you leave here without buying that van. I want to see you leave in that car."

I was speechless and felt adrenaline surge through my body as my fight-or-flight instinct kicked in. I understood that I was being bullied, something I never accepted, even if it meant physical confrontation. I strode toward the door, looked him in the eye, and said, "Move! I am never buying a car from you!"

He hesitated, then stepped out of my way.

As I walked away, he yelled, "I really want to see you leave in that minivan!"

No way in hell.

That was one of my first experiences buying a big-ticket item with the "assistance" of a salesperson, and it was enough to convince me that I would never, under any circumstances, become a salesperson.

Even if that bully of a sales manager hadn't gone so far as to block the door, he should have known better. Asking for the decision to buy before I was ready practically ensured that his ask would be rejected, especially since this was a large, complex sale with plenty at risk—for me anyway. And when he asked again—in the sales business that's referred to as "closing often"—he violated my trust and betrayed his self-orientation. That was the real kiss of death.

ALWAYS BE CLOSING

Self-oriented salespeople are focused on making the sale and getting their commissions. Because of this, they often ask for a commitment to buy before they've earned the right, created enough value for the prospective client, or presented sufficient information for the client to make that commitment. They ignore the prospective client's real concerns and ask for a signature anyway. Some of them even "work" the clients by disclosing the amount of money they stand to gain if they close the deal, or by begging for business by suggesting they'll be fired if they don't close the deal. It's all about them, not the client. Not surprisingly, their prospects do whatever they can to avoid these salespeople.

Starting in the 1930s and continuing up through the 1980s, salespeople were trained to be self-oriented. It wasn't much of a stretch because sales organizations often hired people who were already self-centered and egocentric. They were taught tactics like the "hard sell" and used "tie-downs" like, "Mr. Smith, do you love your wife?" When Smith answered in the affirmative, the salesperson pressed on: "Do you love your children?" When Smith affirmed that he did indeed love his children, the salesperson was ready to pounce. Having just received two "yes" answers in a row and having the prospect sufficiently tied down, he would ask another question that required a "yes" answer, such as, "You do want them to be taken care of should anything happen to you, don't you, Mr. Smith?" Smith, feeling awful about himself, awful about the salesperson, and horribly embarrassed, would quietly and sheepishly whisper, "Yes." The salesperson would then close by saying, "I need you to sign right here so we can take care of your family."

Fortunately, very few salespeople use the hard close now, even though some of the self-orientation persists. Because of these behaviors, laws have been passed to protect buyers who later regret caving into high-pressure sales techniques, allowing them three days to cancel an order. Today, when you make a major purchase like buying a car, you might be asked to sign a document confirming that you weren't abused in any way by the salesperson or the sales process. The dealership wants you to sign to protect the contract, should you later decide that you were pressured. But the negative image lingers of salespeople as being self-oriented, manipulative, and pushy—even though successful salespeople are exactly the opposite.

HOW I GOT INTO SALES

I was one of those people who avoided salespeople whenever possible and thought they were pushy, manipulative, and out for themselves. I never imagined I could go into sales—and never would have if I hadn't been forced into it.

I began my work life as a recruiter in temporary staffing, our family business, where I was taught to look for new business when things were slow. Later, when I took a job in another staffing office, if there was nothing to do, I did what I'd been taught to do in the family business: I spent time calling on companies, scheduling appointments, meeting with their people, and (hopefully) winning their business. I didn't realize that what I was doing was selling. My job title and duties didn't refer to me as a salesperson, and there were three full-time salespeople working with me. I just thought I was helping people who needed my help.

One day, my new manager walked over to my desk and slid a report across the desk.

"Whose accounts are these?" he asked.

When I told him they were mine, he replied, "Good. I want you to cut your hair and go into full-time outside sales."

I was horrified. I was working at that job only so I could front a hard-rock band at night. The thought of cutting my hair was bad enough, but the idea of working in sales was downright repulsive.

"I could never be a salesperson," I told him. "I hate salespeople. They're selfish, manipulative, and pushy, and I'm not any of those things."

My manager, who was very smart, immediately boxed me in with my own words: "Is that how you won all of these clients? By being pushy and manipulative?"

My manager was right. I wasn't acquiring new clients by being pushy or manipulative. I was winning them because I was trying to help them. I understood the challenges they faced and was trying to help them solve their problems. Up until then, my only real experience with salespeople had been with that sales manager at the car lot, and you know how that went. No wonder I had a negative idea about salespeople!

I wouldn't have taken the outside sales job if my manager hadn't threatened to fire me. Fortunately, he went along with me when I made my early sales calls and brought me along on some of his calls as well. And I saw that he was never selfish, manipulative, or pushy. Instead, he was all about finding ways to help his clients get the results they needed. He was the opposite of self-oriented. He was "other oriented," a guy who worked with his clients, not against them. Once I learned this and began to apply it, I started to love sales—and to find success as a salesperson.

HOW DOES YOUR MOTHER SELL?

Occasionally, I teach a class on personal selling at Capital University in Columbus, Ohio. I start by asking the students to shout out words that describe salespeople, and their replies confirm that the negative connotation still exists. I can almost always fill a whiteboard with these words, which almost always include "pushy," "manipulative," "selfish," "money-grubbing," "slick," and "persuasive."

Then I ask them to raise their hands if one of their parents works in sales. Usually 20 percent or more raise their hands. I go on to ask individual students which one of their parents works in sales and wait for someone to say, "It's my mother."

I then reply, "Okay, so tell me what your pushy, selfish, manipulative mother sells."

The others laugh, and the student almost always protests, "My mom is none of those things! Her clients love her! They call her all the time for advice, even on personal issues!"

It's not the ask that makes you a bad salesperson. It never has been. It's the self-orientation.

If you are going to sell well now, if you are going to succeed in sales, you are going to have to ask for commitments. Closing is nonnegotiable. If you aren't willing and able to ask for the commitments you need, you will not succeed in sales. The good news is that nothing about asking requires you to be self-oriented, nor does it demand that you do anything that would violate your client's trust. The old tactical approaches are not necessary, and you won't benefit from using them anyway.

This book is for professional salespeople. It is a book for people who aspire to be their client's trusted advisor. This book is for people who believe in building lifetime relationships on trust, creating value, collaborating, and delivering exceptional results.

This book won't help you if you are looking for tactics that allow you to manipulate, pressure, or trick people into buying from you. This is a book for professionals in the art of selling.

ALWAYS BE CLOSING VERSUS NEVER BE CLOSING

For decades, salespeople were trained to "always be closing"—that is, everything they did was aimed at getting the signature that sealed the deal. But over the last two decades, the world of sales has changed. More competitors have entered the markets. Customers have more choices, have grown more sophisticated in their approach to buying, and have gained power in their relationships with sales organizations. They no longer need to buy from salespeople who bully or badger them with manipulative techniques like the assumptive "either/or" close ("Does Tuesday at ten a.m. work for you, or would Wednesday at two p.m. work better?") or the "take delivery" close ("Would you like your new car in cherry red or in metallic blue?"). A lot of the old approaches deprived prospective clients of choices, and it disempowered them. Selling was something that was being done *to* them. They surely didn't need the help of any salesperson who would use the hard sell to win their business.

Customers started to ignore, avoid, and reject salespeople who used aggressive, self-oriented closing techniques. That's when sales approaches went from the "always be closing" approach to a softer, more consultative style of selling. Then, with the advent of the Internet, social selling, content marketing, and inbound, the pendulum swung all the way to "never be closing"—the idea that selling well means never asking your prospective clients to buy, and allowing them to determine the next steps for themselves. Salespeople now wait passively for their prospects to ask to move the sales process forward. They believe that if they engage well with a prospect, they don't need to ask for the commitments that would move an opportunity forward.

You might be surprised to learn that I subscribe to the "always be closing" approach—just not in pursuit of the commitment to buy, which is what most people were trained to get. Instead, I work toward gaining a series of commitments that advance the sale toward a decision.

In 1988, Neil Rackham wrote one of the legendary books on sales, titled *SPIN Selling*. It stands as one of the best-selling hardcover books that McGraw-Hill has ever published. All these many years later, you can still find *SPIN Selling* in hardcover at your local bookstore. Rackham's book was a methodology for a dialogue between salespeople and their prospective clients. That methodology was powerful then, and it is still highly effective today. The ability to help your prospective client explore the implications of not changing (the *I* in the acronym SPIN) is often enough by itself to help you win deals, because it helps you and your prospective client develop a compelling case for change. But that isn't the part of the book we are going to focus on here. Instead, we are going to focus on the hidden gem in Rackham's work that is almost universally overlooked and ignored.

Leading up to the SPIN model, Rackham carefully and correctly explains that closing behaviors in small, low-risk sales increase the likelihood of acquiring the sale. It makes sense that you ask for the sale early and often when there is little at risk. In these cases, when there is almost no risk of harm in buying, more "asks" are better.

But in larger, complex sales where more is at stake and the risks are higher, closing early and often actually works against the salesperson. Asking for the decision to buy too soon, before the buyer is ready, almost ensures that the salesperson's ask will be rejected. Asking again violates the prospect's trust and betrays the salesperson's self-orientation (a subject about which we will have much more to say later).

Rackham asserts that successful salespeople ask for and obtain certain "advances" that progress toward the final close. Poorly performing salespeople, Rackham found, don't gain these advances. Instead, they settle for indications that the sale will continue (e.g., the customer seems to like the salesperson and is likely to speak with him or her again). But no specific action has been agreed upon to move the sale forward.

Rackham's research didn't suggest "never be closing." In fact, his research showed quite the opposite to be true: It recommended "always be closing," but not for the commitment to buy, which is what most people were trained to get.

Once I read Rackham's work, I applied the idea of gaining a commitment at the end of each interaction, and my sales results immediately improved. This practice alone is transformative, as it is the one thing I have found that keeps deals moving forward. This insight alone has helped me generate literally hundreds of millions of dollars in revenue. That from a book that costs around twenty-five dollars and takes four hours to read.

"Always be closing," as I practice it, involves securing a series of commitments from a prospective client that lead to the decision to buy. Closing happens in stages, each one moving the process forward. In the process, the salesperson becomes the prospective client's trusted advisor and collaborator.

Like Rackham, I've found that the failure to gain these commitments extends the time it takes to close deals and thwarts the salesperson's success, including the financial kind that comes from winning new business. It also deprives the sales organization of revenue and profit, and prospective customers of the results they need, leaving them no better off than they were before. The failure to gain the necessary commitments to move an opportunity forward is also responsible for the death of many deals. Without the commitments, momentum is lost, other priorities get more attention, and both the salesperson and the prospective client lose momentum.

This book is about becoming your clients' trusted advisor by building lifetime relationships based on collaboration, the creation of value, and the delivery of exceptional results by obtaining the commitments necessary for creating and winning opportunities. Not only does the approach work, it is now required in order to succeed in sales.

Today, you need to gain ten specific commitments as you move from the beginning of the sales process to execution. This book is a guide to gaining these ten commitments. By understanding what these commitments are, why you need them, and how to successfully acquire them, you will improve your ability to create and win new opportunities.

A WALK THROUGH THIS BOOK

"Never be closing" is bad advice. It is hurting salespeople and the clients they serve. It is time the pendulum swung back in the other direction, and we are going to give it a good nudge here to start it on its way. It is time to return to "always be closing," but with a more professional and mature view of what "closing" means, and how to ask. For our purposes here, "always be closing" will not mean that we ask for the Commitment to Decide prematurely.

Nothing about "always be closing" will require that you return to the bad practices and tacky techniques that have come to define the stereotypical hard sell. Nothing about "always be closing" means that you have to be self-oriented or that you need to do anything that would betray your client's trust. None of the ideas in this book will cause you to damage your relationship with your prospective client or destroy trust. In fact, the ideas here will transform your relationships and grow your trust.

Absolutely none of the recommendations here will make your prospective clients feel bad about themselves or cause them to feel pressured to make a decision. What your clients will feel instead is the confidence that they are working with a professional who knows what they're doing, has their best interests at heart and is working to help them produce better results.

The ideas contained in this book will help you engage your clients around the sensitive issues that you need to address together to build their better future. These ideas will help you engage with your clients in transformational conversations, the deep discussions of the issues that prevent real change from occurring. It is only through these conversations that your clients can produce those better results, and the commitments here will help guide those conversations.

None of the strategies, tactics, or language choices will have a tacky, embarrassing name. In fact, none of them have a name that does anything more than describe the commitment.

The ideas here will help you develop deeper relationships. They will differentiate you and prove that you are customer-oriented, that you are looking out for your prospective client's interests. The language choices will make you more professional, and you will never feel bad or embarrassed by the words coming out of your mouth.

Let's take a look at what you'll discover in the chapters to come:

Chapter 1: A New Philosophy of Commitment Gaining provides a philosophy for closing or, as we sometimes call it here, commitment gaining. Selling isn't something that you do *to* someone;

instead, it is something you do *for* someone and *with* someone. You will learn why the wrong mindset, skill set, and tool kit prevent you from gaining commitments—and how to use more powerful approaches.

Chapter 2: Control the Commitments and Control the Process lays the groundwork for commitment gaining by describing how buyers really buy, how you can best serve them through that process, and how gaining the ten commitments will ensure that you help your clients produce the results they want and need.

Chapter 3: Trading Value will help you craft a value proposition for each commitment you ask for, trading the value you create in that interaction for your client's commitment. This chapter will help make it easier for your client to say yes to your ask.

Chapter 4: The Commitment for Time will show you how to gain an appointment or meeting with your prospective client. No opportunity is closed without first being opened, so this commitment is a necessary and critical first step. It is also one of the most difficult.

Chapter 5: The Commitment to Explore explains how to gain your prospective client's commitment to explore change. Exploring change will allow you to do the discovery and needs-analysis work that will create opportunities and position you to win them by creating a preference for you, your company, and your solution.

Chapter 6: The Commitment to Change is where opportunities are born. Unless and until your prospective client agrees to change, you won't have a real opportunity. This chapter will help you sort the actual deals in your pipeline from the clutter of nonopportunities.

Chapter 7: The Commitment to Collaborate is all about learning how to ask for—and gain—your prospective client's input, thus creating a partner and allowing the client to own the solution. To make complex sales, you need to collaborate with a prospective client on the solutions that you must develop together.

Chapter 8: The Commitment to Build Consensus is about giving a voice to those who are affected by a decision to change. More decisions are now made democratically. Your prospective client wants and needs the support of the team to move forward. You will learn how to ask for the commitment that moves this process forward by building consensus.

Chapter 9: The Commitment to Invest explains how to ask your prospective clients to invest more to produce the results they need. If your prospective client could get better results at their current investment, they'd already be producing those results and would have no reason to change. You can help them make the necessary investments.

Chapter 10: The Commitment to Review discusses the straightforward ask you must make for the time you need to present your solution. The ask must also include a request that the necessary stakeholders and decision makers be present. This can be a little tricky. You'll leave this chapter prepared to gain a meeting that ensures your solution is 100 percent correct before you ask for the Commitment to Decide.

Chapter 11: The Commitment to Resolve Concerns deals with the fact that most buyers need help handling their fears and doubts as they make major purchases. While most salespeople allow their prospective clients to "get back to them" on their own time, you will ask for the commitment that allows you to be there to serve your dream clients,* guiding them through the resolution of any concerns.

Chapter 12: The Commitment to Decide focuses on what has historically been called "closing." You will learn how to ask for the commitment to buy. This strategy is as straightforward and easy as it gets, and you will be able to master it in minutes.

Chapter 13: The Commitment to Execute looks at the final close, which can be the toughest commitment to gain. It provides the strategies, tactics, and language you need to help your new client produce the results that you sold them. This chapter will help you move from salesperson to trusted advisor.

Chapter 14: Guidelines for Closing will provide you with a set of ideas to help you diagnose some of the challenges you might have gaining commitments and some changes you may need to make.

Chapter 15: Transformational Conversations and Fearing the Wrong Dangers will guide you through helping your dream client overcome cold feet by directing their attention to the real business dangers and the value they stand to gain by moving forward.

---

* A "dream client" is the prospective client from whom you can create breathtaking, jaw-dropping, earth-shattering value and who will allow you to capture some of that value in the form of a higher price.

Chapter 16: Managing Commitments provides a set of ideas that will help you manage your sales opportunities by ensuring that the commitments necessary to win an opportunity are being gained.

In the closing chapter, I share my thoughts on why all of this matters now more than ever, and who you have to become to sell effectively today.

Now I'd like to ask you for thirty minutes of your time in which I will share with you a philosophy of closing that you can immediately put to work improving your sales game. What do you look like over the next half hour for a quick run-through of a big idea that will help you make sales?

Chapter 1

A NEW PHILOSOPHY OF COMMITMENT GAINING

TO SELL EFFECTIVELY, YOU NEED A PHILOSOPHY. NOT THE ACademic kind of philosophy that they teach in universities. You need a practical philosophy, like the Greeks practiced. The Greeks didn't just argue about philosophy in theory. They practiced philosophy.

If you were an Epicurean, you ate and drank because that was what a good life was made up of: pleasure. If you were a Stoic (a very popular idea now, by the way), you endured the hardships of life without complaint. Philosophy was about living in a way that was in line with what you believed. A philosophy should guide how you sell too.

Here's my philosophy, and it is a major thread that runs throughout this book: Selling isn't something you do *to* someone. It is something you do *for* someone and *with* someone.

If you want to be a consultative salesperson and a trusted advisor, this is the starting point in earning that moniker.

CAVEAT EMPTOR

Caveat emptor is Latin for "let the buyer beware," a general philosophy of sales dating to the time that people first started trading. It emphasizes the buyer's responsibility to protect himself from the merchant (read: salesperson). If you struck a bad deal, then it was your fault. You should have known better. How could you have let yourself get duped when you knew that merchants were always trying to put one over on you? *Caveat emptor* was a necessary philosophy because, for most of human history, selling was something that one person did to another. To this day, we still use the expression "you sold them." You "sold them" on your ideas or your product. Taking advantage of the rubes, you "sold them a bill of goods," parting them from their money without delivering the promised value. The idea of *caveat emptor* made it clear that the seller was acting for his own gain or for his company's benefit, or both. There was little indication that any selling was done for the benefit of the buyer.

Fortunately, times have changed. Because your clients have so many choices available to them, and because word of mouth has been amplified by the Internet and social media, *caveat venditor* is a more apt philosophy today. *Caveat venditor* means "let the seller beware." This is a good change, as it has suppressed a lot of bad sales behaviors. Now if a seller takes advantage of you, you can share your unhappy experience with your friends, family, and countless strangers on social media and various review sites. For today's sellers, the potential penalty for being self-oriented, manipulative, unfair, or deceitful is too high. One sale isn't worth the loss of countless future sales—something good sales organizations and salespeople have always known.

In truth, most salespeople don't want to take advantage of other people. Most people don't want to perform work that makes them feel bad about themselves or would make them guilty of harming others. And they don't have to. Sales can be a very rewarding career because, properly done, it requires that you help people get results they couldn't have achieved without you. And by doing so, you can develop deep, lasting, valuable relationships. Thus, selling isn't something you do *to* someone. Instead, you work *with* your clients, using your resourcefulness and initiative to create opportunities or possibilities for better outcomes. At your very best, you and your clients become strategic partners. You become your client's trusted advisor, a title you must earn and re-earn by consistently offering sound advice, by knowing and communicating what needs to happen for your client to produce better results.

THE RIGHT MINDSET

How do you learn to embrace *caveat venditor*? Not to do it simply because that's what's currently being done in sales, but to really take it to heart? You start by developing the right mindset. Indeed, your mindset is one of the major determining factors of your success. The right mindset makes commitment gaining easier because your underlying beliefs are healthy and empowering. The six key components of the right mindset are confidence, caring, persistence, speaking from the client's mind, embracing concerns, and realizing it's not about you.

Confidence

Confidence—in yourself as well as in what you're selling—allows you to act with your customer's best interests at heart. Confidence permits you to ask a prospective client for the commitment to take the next step. It comes from the belief that *you can and will make a difference for that client, and you will be able to deliver the outcomes they need.* If you don't embrace these beliefs, your lack of confidence will show and will prevent you from gaining commitments.

Naturally, you won't feel confident that you'll make a positive difference for your client unless you believe in your product, service, or solution. If you aren't 100 percent sure about what you sell, your prospective client will sense the incongruity between what you say and what she sees. You may come across as being inauthentic, or seem like you aren't telling the truth or aren't sure about what you're saying. In short, if *you* don't really believe that your product is so great that your prospects must commit to the next step in the process, neither will they.

Let's take a quick look at what causes you to lose confidence and how you maintain it. Confidence in your product, service, solution, and company doesn't come from believing that your clients will never have problems. Instead, it comes from your understanding that no company delivers exceptional results without being able to effectively deal with the day-to-day challenges of executing. Even more important to maintaining your confidence is your belief that you are going to make a difference for your clients, and that you will be there to make sure they are taken care of when they have the inevitable challenges that come with real change initiatives.

Caring

Caring is the root of trust, and trust is the foundation of all relationships—including commercial relationships. Caring is what makes you other-oriented instead of self-oriented. This isn't the soft stuff in business; it's the hard stuff. All things being equal, relationships win. All things being unequal, relationships still win. Your job in sales is to make all things unequal by creating relationships of value. That means more than liking your client or having a personal relationship, even though both of these are extremely helpful in creating a preference for you, your company, and your solution. "Relationships of value" means that you create value for your clients as someone who provides ideas and advice—and who also ensures that the outcomes they sell are delivered.

You make selling more difficult when you are focused on "making the sale." That outcome is about what you want and what you'll receive for having won the deal. That inward focus prevents you from being effective in selling.

When you care about helping other people generate the results that they can't generate without you, your outward focus is part of what creates a preference and makes you easier to buy from. When your focus is on helping your dream clients make the changes that they need to make, gaining the commitments necessary to move forward—and eventually the commitment to buy from you—becomes natural and easy.

This is a mindset shift for most salespeople. Too often, they focus on booking appointments with potential clients that they can report to the sales manager when asked. You could instead focus on sharing information and ideas that would help prospective clients understand why they need to change now. Too often, salespeople focus on "pushing" their product or service rather than engaging with the prospective client in producing better results through change. Too often, they focus on winning deals. But what if, instead, you focused on helping the client "win"? Truth be told, their win is your win—in that order.

Persistence

This is a book about commitment gaining in the complex sale. Sales is now all about helping people change, but change isn't easy. You are going to have to be persistent. I mean really, really persistent.

You are going to ask for commitments that your prospective clients will refuse to make. They are going to fear change—even when they know it is necessary. Your dream clients will refuse the commitments that move them closer to the results they need, even when doing so hurts their company. They'll also fail to keep commitments, even though they had every intention of honoring them. Look, if this were easy, you wouldn't need this book.

You are going to have to persist in asking for and gaining the commitments you will need to help your dream clients move from their current state to the better future state available to them. You're going to hear no, and know that you'll have to try again. You are also going to have meetings canceled, voice mails and e-mails unreturned, and prospects who drag their feet through the process. Do not be deterred. As Benjamin Franklin said, "Energy and persistence conquer all things."

Speaking from the Client's Mind

Great salespeople make great language choices. They have the right words for each situation, words that can work a kind of magic. That's why sales is more of an art than a science.

Many salespeople eagerly memorize the latest, greatest "selling words" and "selling phrases," convinced that having these on the tip of the tongue is the key to success. This means they're thinking of language as a tool to be mastered and used to hammer home sales, rather than as a means of developing great relationships with potential clients, of encouraging the flow of ideas as you build toward a better future.

It is certainly important to be well versed in the words and phrases used by potential clients when speaking of the technical aspects of their business. But it is just as important to keep your mind focused on the client's needs, challenges, and goals when communicating with him. Before speaking up, take a moment to think of the client's challenges and goals. Mentally make them your own, then speak. Now that you are speaking, in a sense, "from your client's mind," you will naturally communicate your desire to help him succeed. The actual words you use are less important than communicating this desire.

There's no set formula for selecting the right words, but here's a rule of thumb: If the language you use makes you feel bad about yourself, if it feels tricky or coercive in any way, you're not speaking from your client's mind. You're speaking from your own desire to win the sale. When you are self-oriented, your intentions and your words betray you.

I am not saying that working your way through the sales process won't sometimes make some of your prospective clients uncomfortable. No doubt they will sometimes have to face unpleasant facts. And you will likely have to present this unhappy data to get them to realize that it is time to make a major change. But when you fix your mind on helping your client before you speak, your words will be much more powerful.

You acquire good language choices in a couple of different ways. Sometimes you are lucky enough to work with a peer or manager who happens to have an excellent command of language, because he or she speaks from the client's mind. You can learn a lot by considering carefully what you hear and by practicing thinking in such a way that similar language flows easily from your lips. In fact, if people on your team make great language choices, ask to join them on sales calls so you can absorb not just the words they use, but the mindset they adopt to produce those words.

The nice thing about the dynamic human interaction that is a sales call is that, if you listen well, you can receive immediate feedback as to whether what you are doing is working. You can literally see the impact it is making, good or bad, in real time. You can use that real-time feedback to make adjustments as you strive to develop the right communication mindset.

Embracing Concerns

The very act of asking for commitments means that you are going to hear the word "no" more often than you would like. That's why "overcoming objections" is one of the major skills salespeople have long been taught. That language hasn't really kept up with the evolution of sales. A healthier and more accurate description of what successful salespeople do is "embrace and resolve concerns."

An objection is a disagreement; it's a negative thing we want to avoid. Just thinking of the word "objection" when a prospect expresses concerns can make you feel as if you have to "win" the conversation. When that happens, you might perceive your dream client's expression of a very real concern as a challenge, a battle of wills. By changing your perception, by seeing an "objection" as a real concern worth addressing, you can change your mindset and change your approach. You can be curious and work to understand the source of that objection.

As you will learn later in this book, your prospective clients often fear the wrong danger. If you don't, can't, or won't embrace and address their concerns and fears, they are justified in resisting moving forward. Why would you ever agree to something that you don't feel is in your best interest? Why, then, should you ever expect your clients to?

Helping your prospective clients deal with their fears, real or imagined, is how salespeople help their clients change. This change is what is always necessary for producing greater results. If your dream clients could get the results they need without doing something different, they'd already be producing those results.

Salespeople struggle when they don't know how to respond when their prospective client says no. Don't struggle: Embrace and resolve.

Realizing It's Not About You

The better you understand your prospective client's point of view, desires, and needs, the more effectively you can help them reach their goals and the more trust you can build in your relationship. Conversely, if you don't know what they're struggling to achieve, if you don't understand their point of view, how can you know what to offer them? And why should they believe anything you have to say, or even agree to a meeting in the first place? To be an effective salesperson, you need to look at the world through your client's eyes, to adopt their perspective.

Make no mistake about it: Being other-oriented is a powerful mindset, for we are naturally self-oriented beings. But this skill can be developed. You can learn to take the perspective of "other" and look at things through your dream client's eyes. Begin by asking yourself:

- If you were your dream client, what might you be struggling to achieve?
- What would you be concerned about when considering what the salesperson is offering?
- What would compel you to say yes to the request for a meeting?
- What would the value proposition need to be for you to agree to spend your limited time meeting with someone you know is going to try to sell you something?
- What aren't you currently getting from other salespeople? What might make you want to jump ship and start buying from another salesperson or company?

In my workshops, I've found that salespeople, sales managers, and sales leaders often struggle to take on the perspective of their clients and prospects. We spend so much of our time focused on the challenge of acquiring clients and selling well that it's easy to forget that clients have their own perspectives. We also tend to underestimate the consequences of the commitments we ask them to make, which may include firing an old friend they've been buying from for years.

The more you can look through your dream clients' eyes and see their perspective, the easier it will be for you to help them make the decisions and changes necessary to produce better results. The more other-oriented you become, the more your prospective clients will feel that you understand their needs and are dedicated to serving them.

Thus, no part of the sales process can be about you or what you need. Every commitment you ask for must be about what your prospective client needs in order to produce better results, overcome obstacles, and create a better future.

I'll repeat this, because it is so important: **No part of the sales process can be about you or what you need. Selling isn't something you do *to* someone. It is something you do *for* someone and *with* someone.**

Now that you have a powerful philosophy to support the rest of what follows in this book, can I ask you to turn the page so I can share with you some powerful ideas about controlling the sales process, one of the two big things you are going to need before we get into the commitments?

Chapter 2

CONTROL THE COMMITMENTS AND CONTROL THE PROCESS

AS SALESPEOPLE, WE FOLLOW A SALES PROCESS. THIS USUALLY starts with targeting, moves to qualifying, then into discovery, followed by a presentation, negotiation, and close. Your sales process may have more steps, or it may have fewer, depending on what and how you sell.

Buyers also follow a process. For our purposes here, we are not looking at arm's-length processes that purchasing departments create, the type of process you know as an RFP or "request for proposal." These processes are designed to prevent a salesperson from creating a preference and, in most cases, limit your ability to do the work of making change.

We're also not talking about the general buying decision process that starts with problem recognition and includes the information search, evaluation of alternatives, and purchase decision. We need to go a bit deeper than this to understand how buyers think and feel so we can understand how to best serve them in the process of changing. In other words, we want to understand the buyer's psychology. This begins with the understanding that your dream clients don't have a map. They *are* the map.

Your prospective clients look at the process of change subjectively, not objectively. They aren't probing their own psychology to understand why they feel the way they feel or why they want what they want. In many cases, they aren't even aware of the fact that they resist change, that they protect the status quo, and that their fears prevent them from improving what they are doing. Just as you're unaware of your own blind spots, your prospective clients are unaware of theirs.

Always remember that your buyers don't have a "buying process map" they follow in the way you follow your sales process. They don't have a list of outcomes they need to achieve so they can make good buying decisions, and they don't have neatly drawn charts that segment their journey in stages. Again, they don't have this map, because they *are* the map.

What your dream client wants is for problems to be solved, challenges overcome, opportunities pursued, and greater outcomes obtained. They do what they do when buying because they believe they have to in order to accomplish what they want or need. Let's look at how buyers really engage in the process of change and what their real process looks like.

THE PSYCHOLOGY OF HOW BUYERS REALLY BUY

Dissonance

Think back on the last time you bought something expensive, perhaps a new automobile or a house. Unless this purchase was triggered by some event that made it absolutely necessary that you buy on the spot, you likely didn't decide to make that decision in a single day. It's more likely true that the desire and need built over time. For example, your previous car had maintenance issues. It no longer met your expectations, and you didn't want to keep putting money into it. But even though you knew you could buy a new car that met all your needs, you did just enough to keep it puttering along—since you hadn't decided to give up on it just yet. So even though you had a compelling reason to change, you were making it work.

The challenge for most of us in sales is that we recognize our dream clients have a compelling reason to change long before they do. We've developed the insights that have allowed us to create new products, new solutions, and new services designed to help our clients produce greater results, in many cases before they have even recognized their need for these new capabilities. You can undoubtedly call to mind some dream clients you know would benefit from what you sell, even though they resist your attempts to schedule a meeting. You can also describe the very reasons they should change now, as well as the economic, technological, scientific, and cultural changes that are going to force them to change eventually, whether they like it or not. But still, they cling to what they've been doing.

In one of my staffing businesses, the economic and labor market trends that impact my clients are easily discernible long before they become serious. Even as their ability to recruit and hire the talent they need deteriorates, they hold fast to the idea that they can keep doing what they've always done. They're not yet dissatisfied enough to act.

The reality of sales is that most buyers don't feel compelled to change when you are prospecting, trying to obtain the Commitment for Time and the Commitment to Explore. Instead, they're experiencing a sort of dissonance, the feeling that something is off, that it isn't quite right. Even though things aren't working exactly the way they need them to, they find ways to work around their challenges, becoming more frustrated at the effort it takes to get things done.

You, as a consultative salesperson, need to understand the source of your dream clients' dissonance to help them understand it. It may be that the assumptions underlying the prospect's business model are no longer valid, but they don't yet fully understand this fact. It might be that changes in the economic climate are producing changes for their clients, changes they haven't yet responded to. It might be that scientific, technological, or cultural developments are making it harder for them to do what they once did easily, and they don't yet understand why. These changes are all part and parcel of living in a time of accelerating disruptive change, and as painful as they may be, they provide opportunity—for you and for your dream clients.

When you understand the source of your prospective clients' dissonance, you can help them develop it into a problem worth solving. Helping them develop that dissonance into a problem worth solving is how you create value for your clients.* If you want to be a trusted advisor and a consultative salesperson, you can't wait until your dream client experiences the negative impact of *not* changing before you decide to help them. You have to be helping them proactively, and that means helping them understand the need to change.

To do this, you'll need to gain control of the process by getting the commitments that allow you to help them turn their dissonance into a problem worth solving, into a compelling reason to change. To do this, you'll need to learn how to gain the Commitment for Time and the Commitment to Explore, which are discussed in Chapters 4 and 5, respectively. These commitments allow you to control the process and better serve your prospective clients.

A Problem Worth Solving

In the past, we talked about buyers being dissatisfied, and while there is still some value to this concept, the word "dissatisfaction" no longer

---

* If you are unsure how to understand the trends and factors that would be causing your dream client to change, go back and read Chapter 16: Business Acumen in *The Only Sales Guide You'll Ever Need.*

covers enough ground. This is because plenty of your dream clients are dissatisfied about all sorts of things, but they don't find their dissatisfaction compelling enough to do anything about it. It's also true that they don't believe they have the bandwidth to change, and their problems aren't a big enough priority to command their limited time, energy, and resources. The status quo, when deeply entrenched, is a tough obstacle to break through.

I've called on clients who were struggling to produce the results they promised their clients and were seriously concerned about losing them. They were clearly worried and in dire straits, yet still not dissatisfied enough to change. You've likely called on prospective clients for whom things had gone so bad for so long that they knew their current state was not good. They switched from one provider to the next, hoping things would change. When nothing changed, they accepted that this was just how things worked. They lowered their standards and learned to live with a status quo that no longer served them.

It's wonderful when you find a prospective client that already believes they have a compelling reason to change. Its better still when you've nurtured the relationships so well that you are the first and only call your dream client makes when they recognize a compelling reason to change. Unfortunately, the reality is that most of the time we find our dream clients in the stage of dissonance, and we have to help them discover a problem they believe is worth solving.

To move your dream client from dissonance to believing they have a problem worth solving, you have to help them find a compelling reason to change.

Compelling Change

The single most frequent question salespeople ask me is: "How can I be more compelling?" What they are really asking is how they can turn the dissonance into a commitment to act. To compel someone to change, you have to leverage what's already—or what should be—compelling him to change. Ask yourself:

- What problems or challenges is your dream client allowing to persist that, if changed, would radically improve their results?
- What do they lose by not making these changes? Is it money? Clients? Market share?
- What legislative, economic, cultural, or scientific trends will negatively impact your prospective client's results in the future and harm their business? Which of these trends provide opportunities?

Note that there is nothing about your company, your products, or your solutions in these questions. As good as your product or service is, it does not provide your dream client with a compelling reason to change by itself. Your real concern is getting your dream client to recognize that the dissonance they have been suffering through is actually a compelling reason to change. What you sell comes later, as the solution to their challenges.

Sometimes your prospective clients don't even know something is wrong. They have not yet reached the stage of dissonance—but you can still help them find a powerful reason to change. I once had a prospect who was massively underperforming when it came to the service my company sold. Without suggesting that he was doing anything wrong, I showed him the results other companies were producing as part of an executive summary. Being a competitive guy, he was immediately motivated to close the gap. Until he saw what the competition was doing, he didn't know he should be dissatisfied.

Once your prospective clients realize that they have a compelling reason to change, they start to work to discover the cause or condition that needs to change, and to explore ideas about what that change would require.*

You control this process by gaining the Commitment to Explore and the Commitment to Change. Without these commitments, your dream clients will remain just that: a dream.

Possibilities, Options, Alternatives, and Choices

Once prospective clients decide they have a compelling reason to change and develop some idea about what they need, they want to explore possibilities. They want to weigh their options against one another and to explore the trade-offs that would come with one solution or another. They then want to collaborate on building the plan, process, and solution that moves them from their current state to their desired future state.

You can control the process here by providing different ideas about what might work, collaborating with your contacts to fine-tune what they believe might work, building consensus around a solution, and reviewing proposed solutions. You serve them by providing them with possibilities and options, and you help them understand the trade-offs they may need to make. If you don't help them explore choices in this manner, they will look to your competitors to provide them with options in an attempt to meet their needs.

The truth is, clients can produce just about any result they want, provided they invest enough time, money, and resources. Your dream clients, however, don't have an unlimited budget. That's why the

---

* If you need help with this, go back to *The Only Sales Guide You'll Ever Need* and read Chapter 14: Diagnosing. That will help you find the root cause of what needs to change, as well as the ground truth about its real impact on your dream client's business.

Commitment to Invest should come earlier in the buying process than most salespeople realize. Money is often the limiting factor. Having this conversation before you present your solution helps ensure that you present something your dream client *can* say yes to, and that you don't have to do too much negotiating later.

The Commitments to Collaborate, Build Consensus, Invest, and Review are all important for controlling the process and helping your dream client create a better future. You will learn to control the process by gaining these commitments in Chapters 7 through 10.

Assessing Risks, Resolving Concerns, and Addressing Fears

During the final stage of the buyer's journey, buyers generally ask for time to think through their decisions on their own. They have fears, even if they wouldn't describe them using that word.

In this stage of their process, they want to assess their risks to ensure the decision to change is the right one, and that the partner they are considering is the right partner. They also want to resolve their concerns, ensuring that they are making the right choice and not overlooking anything. Although your dream client won't say, "I am afraid of what might go wrong," their request for time to "think about it" tells you that something is indeed wrong.

Allowing your prospective client to run off to assess the risks, resolve their concerns, and address their own fears is a poor strategy. Giving them more time to stew in their concerns doesn't serve them; time by itself has never helped anyone make a better decision. Only more information, better counsel, and an opportunity to process information effectively allows risks to be addressed, concerns to be resolved, and fears to be overcome.

You serve your dream client here by gaining the Commitment to Resolve Concerns, something we will cover in depth in Chapter 11. By controlling the process here, you make it easier to gain the Commitment to Decide (Chapter 12).

You serve your dream client when you control the process. That said, let me be clear about this: You control the process, but you don't control the outcome. Controlling the process allows you to serve your dream client, to give them what they need to make good decisions. To control the outcome, you would have to use old-school tactics like tie-downs and other self-oriented and trust-destroying tactics. Nothing you do guarantees the outcome that your dream client changes and that you win.

Trying to control the outcome doesn't serve the client. Controlling the process massively stacks the deck in your favor by increasing the odds that you help your prospect decide to change and chooses you as the partner to help them.

When Buyers Control the Process

When a buyer does have a formal buying process, a request for proposal, it will be difficult for you to win their business. Selling is about conversations around value and commitment gaining. It's also about creating a preference for your solution, and for you. You are trying to be consultative and become a trusted advisor, an integral part of your client's extended management team. That can't happen when the prospect has a formal request for proposal process, which is why so many sales organizations do not respond to the RFP. It's difficult to have conversations around value because of the arm's-length nature of the buyer's formal process. The RFP process starts at possibilities, options, and trade-offs, way past the point where salespeople create the most value. Everyone looks the same on a response to an RFP, leaving only price as a factor where real differences are found.

As you look at all the commitments that are necessary to win a complex sale, you'll notice that most of them are missing in a formal buying process. A commitment of time has been eliminated. A commitment to explore the current state, as well as the future state, has been eliminated because the buyers believe they've already done that work on their own. Other commitments, including an opportunity to review proposals before submitting, have been completely eliminated.

Because the buyers have a formal process, it's difficult for a sales organization to serve them well. Remember, however, selling isn't something you do to someone. It is something you do for someone and with someone. But you can't do something for and with someone if they won't let you.

When a company employs a buying process, it doesn't often serve them well either. They prevent themselves from having conversations with salespeople who have already dealt with similar challenges and opportunities in other companies. This gives the salespeople much greater "situational knowledge" than any individual company has, because they have seen many variations of what works and what doesn't.

More still, many of the stakeholders within the buyer's company never get an opportunity to vet their potential partners themselves, to have their voices heard, or to share what's most important to creating and generating new and better results with a potential new partner. This can create resistance to working with a new partner, and it can make the execution much more difficult, especially when the stakeholders have been given only a one-hour presentation in which to determine who they believe is going to make the best partner. They're getting married after a single, relatively lousy date. Is it any wonder they don't get the partner they need?

When buyers skip stages that are necessary in developing an understanding, developing relationships, and collaborating on a solution, they usually end up disappointed.

The best advice I can give you for responding to an RFP is to call the purchasing people and push back, telling them all the things in their request that are going to prevent them from achieving the results they are pursuing. This is how you create dissonance, and you create the need for them to do more discovery. Once they start asking questions about what's wrong with their approach, you become a value creator, and you have a reasonably good chance of creating a preference.

If, for any reason, you are afraid that pointing out the problems in their document might cause you to lose the RFP, know that you have almost certainly already lost it. Most RFPs require that all respondents agree to their terms, leaving only price as the differentiator.

Skipping Commitments

Buyers often ask salespeople to skip stages in the sales process. This may have happened to you. Have you ever received a call from a prospective client who asks you to send your pricing and a proposal without ever having met you? This means they've skipped a number of stages and a number of the necessary commitments that allow you to ensure they get the new results they need.

For example, many buyers attempt to skip the process of building consensus within their own organization. They forbid the salesperson from speaking to other stakeholders, even though without their support the initiative will either die or be much more difficult to execute.

It is important to control the process and not let the buyer skip commitments. This is the best way to serve your prospective client as a trusted advisor and create a preference for you, your company, and your solution.

Buyers aren't the only ones who try to skip necessary commitments. Salespeople often skip gaining the commitments they need because they are afraid asking for the commitments will make the opportunity more difficult to win. But this is not true: Skipping commitments makes it less likely that you'll win that opportunity. Here's a quick example. You know you need a commitment to meet the other stakeholders so you can develop consensus around the solution. You also know that one or two of those stakeholders is likely to be an obstacle. So you avoid asking for those meetings, hoping against hope that the stakeholders who oppose change will stand down and allow a decision to be made for the good of the company. What's more likely to happen is that this ignored stakeholder's resistance will prevent you from building consensus and cause a "no decision," where the buyer decides to live with the dissonance of the status quo.

Buyers typically do not have a buying process, and when they do it's not an effective one. This means it is up to us, the salespeople, to gain the commitments necessary to helping our prospective clients change. You have to serve the buyer at every stage of this process, even when they don't want to agree to make the necessary commitments that would serve the outcomes they need. If you can't get that agreement, you probably can't help them.

Gaining Commitments

Much of this book is about gaining the commitments to help prospective clients move from their current state to a future state in an efficient and effective process. This means we are trying to create a process that serves our dream clients and our companies. It also means that we have to first gain the commitment as to what the process needs to be.

To succeed in this mission, you need to go from commitment to commitment, always explaining the value of taking the next step together, always overcoming your prospective client's fears and concerns, and always working to nudge things forward, even when there is resistance to doing so.

Now that you know that you are going to have to control the process to help your dream clients change, the next best step for us to take together is to spend a little time talking about another important concept: trading value. Can we move into the next chapter so I can provide you with a critical concept for producing better results faster by making your ask irresistible?

Chapter 3

TRADING VALUE

TO GAIN THE COMMITMENTS YOU NEED TO CONTROL THE PRO-
cess, you are going to have to trade something of value. Trading value
is a critical concept in commitment gaining, and we have to cover it
here, before we get to the actual commitments. What it means to "trade
value" is that you promise your prospective client something of equal
or greater value in exchange for the commitment you are asking for. It's
easy to understand this concept by looking at examples.

When calling to schedule an appointment with their dream client,
some salespeople say something like, "I'd like to stop by and introduce
myself and my services and learn about your business."

This language still works sometimes, but let's look at the value proposition for your prospective client. They get the great honor of meeting
a salesperson who promises to talk about themselves and their business,
probably using a slide deck with pictures of their management team,
their locations, and the logos of their well-recognized clients. Addition-
ally, they get to answer the salesperson's questions about their business.
The very same questions every salesperson has asked them in every past
meeting they've agreed to.

Can you see why it's so easy for your dream client to contain their enthusiasm? The lack of a value proposition for the sales call makes this an easy commitment to reject. There is no real value for your dream client in this pitch. Their time is too valuable to waste on something with no return on the investment.

What value could you trade for that meeting? What could you give your prospective client in exchange for their time that would benefit them—whether or not they ever do business with you in the future? That ask might sound different.

"I am calling you to schedule a time to share with you the four trends that are going to impact your business over the next twelve to eighteen months, and some ideas about the decisions these trends might require you to take. Even if you never work with us, you'll ask your team different questions, and you'll have some ideas about what you need do."

This is a better value proposition. You are trading something with potential value. In this case, your dream client is going to learn about the four trends that may potentially harm or benefit their business, and they are going to have new questions and ideas to share with their team as they discuss these issues. As an added bonus, you've acknowledged that your prospective client receives this value even if they never work with you.

This principle runs through every commitment you will ever ask for, including each of the ten included in this book. Every commitment you ask your dream client to make needs to create value for them, and it is your job to explain or remind them of what that value is.

COMMITMENTS CREATE VALUE FOR YOUR DREAM CLIENTS

You know that in sales it is better to be other-oriented than self-oriented. The more you focus on the people you are trying to help, the easier selling is. The more you focus on what you want, the more difficult it is to sell. This is especially true of closing.

When you ask to introduce yourself and your company, your outcome is very clear: You want to try to sell your dream client whatever it is you sell. In the second example above, it is clear that you are trying to do something that will benefit your prospective client—even if they never buy from you. There is no question about your other-orientation here because you have promised the value whether or not your client ever buys from you.

You would never say, "I'd really like to see you buy from me because the commission I make off you is going to pay for my vacation!" Fortunately, almost no one would say something so overtly self-oriented. That said, most people make a mistake that, while not as awful as being self-oriented, still makes closing for commitments difficult: They say nothing about the value the client receives by saying yes to the commitment.

You may have said something like, "I'd like to schedule a meeting to come back and explore this issue more. What do you look like next week?" That's not horrible, but it doesn't tell your dream client what they get for their investment of time. The client is thinking, "More questions? Where is all this going? What are we doing here?" They wouldn't have to ask themselves those questions if you explained why you were asking for this commitment and what they stood to gain by agreeing to it.

"I'd like to come back and explore the root cause of this issue and explore what might be necessary to improve it and what some of your choices might be later. We'll both have a better idea of what makes sense and what we might do about it together, if anything."

What does your dream client get here? They get to discover the root cause of their presenting problem. They also get to explore what they might need to do to improve their results, and they get to explore some of their choices. They have a clear idea of what they are getting in return for their time.

There is a pro tip in that language that you may not have picked up. At the end, I added, "if anything." That language is there to lower the commitment level. One of the reasons your prospective clients avoid meetings with salespeople and go dark during the sales process is because they feel they are being pressured to make the Commitment to Decide, a decision that often comes much later in the process. When you remind them that they are not ready to make this commitment, you eliminate the feeling of being pressured. It lets your prospective clients know that they have some control, and it prevents them from feeling like they are being controlled.

Every commitment you ask for must create value for your dream client. If this sounds soft to you, know that what is good for your prospective client is automatically good for you. If you trade real value for every commitment, you are creating a preference for you, for your company, and for your solution—a theme that we will repeat throughout this book.

WEAK AND STRONG

You now know that every sales interaction needs to have its own value proposition, but some value propositions are stronger than others. The stronger the value proposition, the easier it is to gain the commitment you are asking your prospective client to make. The weaker the value proposition, the more difficult it is to gain that commitment.

"I'd like to come back and learn a little more about you and your company. Can we meet next Thursday at two p.m.?" This is a weak value proposition. It doesn't say anything about what is going to be accomplished in that meeting that is going to benefit the prospective client.

- Why do you want to learn more about the person and their company?
- What are you going to do with the information you gain that will help them later?
- How does your dream client know that you aren't going to waste their time?

This may work from time to time, but it's a weak value proposition. The weaker the value proposition, the easier it is for your dream client to reject. That rejection is feedback that what you are doing isn't working. You need to take that feedback and adjust your approach. If you want a different result, you have to do something different, something that creates a different outcome.

"I'd like to schedule a meeting to come back and learn more about the challenge you are having right now so I can get a better understanding of what some of your choices might be. I'll be prepared to share some things that we've done to help other people with similar challenges to explore what might make sense for you. What does Thursday look like?"

Why do you want to learn more? So you can understand the issues or challenges or opportunities enough to provide some potential course of action.

What are you going to do with that information that will help them later? You are going to share with them what you've done to help other people, giving them some ideas of what they might do, whether or not they ever buy from you.

This is a stronger value proposition. It's more difficult to say no to because it describes what is to be gained by saying yes.

YOUR RESPONSIBILITY

You want to control the process so you can better serve your dream client. You are going to exercise control over that process by gaining the commitments that allow you to do everything necessary to help your dream client change what they are doing now and produce the better results they need. You gain those commitments by trading future value for the commitments you are asking your prospective client to make.

It's your responsibility to know what commitment your dream client needs to make and why they need to make it. It's your responsibility to understand what value is being created for them by agreeing to move forward. You are also responsible for explaining your strong value proposition in terms your dream client can understand and agree to.

As far as I know, no one has ever written a closing book like this one. Before now, no one has outlined all the commitments you need to ask for and obtain as you sell. Many salespeople don't know what commitments they need, so most of your prospective clients won't have been asked to make many of the commitments in this book, and so they are unaware of what commitments would truly serve them. That's why it is critical to your success that you can explain the value you are creating in exchange for that commitment.

Your prospective client may not know why you are asking them to commit to collaborating with them. The salespeople who called on them before walked in and proposed their solution, believing that was the right thing to do. These same salespeople were single-threaded, calling on one contact they believed was their "champion" or "power sponsor," not recognizing that the decision was going to be made by stakeholders they didn't even know existed. That makes it your responsibility to know what needs to be done next and why. Many of your clients will never have been asked to make many of the commitments in this book, at least overtly. Very few will know what needs to happen to move from their current state to a better future state.

The Value You Trade

Let's look at the value you trade when asking for each of the ten commitments.

Time: When you ask your dream client to give you their time, you have to give them equal value in insights and ideas that help them produce better results. This requires that you have the business acumen and situational knowledge to create that value for them during every sales interaction.

Exploration: Your dream client's commitment to explore change requires that you provide them with a deeper understanding of what is at the heart of why they are experiencing dissonance and why they should change. To do so, you are going to need to have an approach to discovery that allows you to do the consultative work of uncovering the real issues and obstacles to better performance.

Change: Asking for the Commitment to Change is a big deal. It is one of the most difficult commitments to gain. The value you trade here is a vision of a better future and how you are going to help your dream client get there. This commitment requires that you have the courage to have candid conversations about the process of change. Even when it is uncomfortable.

Collaboration: The value you exchange for the opportunity to collaborate is that your dream client gets a solution that is tailored to their needs. To help them get what is going to work for them, you have to be willing to initiate a process that brings their specific needs to light, and to make the necessary adjustments to the solution you are going to later propose.

Consensus: You provide value here by helping your dream client create the alignment necessary to prevent them from having their change initiative die a premature death from lack of consensus. You're going to need exceptional empathy, emotional intelligence, negotiating skills, and the ability to help people make trade-offs that mitigate the challenges that come with change.

Investment: A lot of people inside your dream client's company know that they are underinvesting. They want to spend more money to solve their problem, but they may not have had the experience of working with a salesperson who can help them justify paying more. You are trading a partner who can help them make the case for a greater investment inside their company and justify the delta between the investment you are asking for and the alternatives.

Review: The value you are trading here is an opportunity to make changes and modifications to what you are building with your prospective client. It also prevents them from having people on their team kill a deal because it didn't address their needs. You must possess the ability to control the process and make the changes that get you to yes.

Resolving concerns: You trade the opportunity to have professional help assessing risks, resolving concerns, and addressing fears and the certainty that your dream client's change initiative will succeed. You need the ability to elicit and understand your dream client's concerns and the ability to assuage their fears.

Deciding: You celebrate when you win. But does your dream client? The value you trade for the Commitment to Decide is the better future you have promised your dream client. They also get a new strategic partner who is going to ensure they succeed.

Execution: This is where the rubber meets the road. You are going to trade the value of having a partner who is there to help do the heavy lifting in exchange for making the changes necessary to produce better results.

These ten commitments are an upward spiral of greater and greater value creation. Each commitment builds on the prior commitments, moving your dream client closer to the better future you are helping them create.

A NOTE ON OTHER-ORIENTATION

Your intention in sales must have an "other-orientation." That other-orientation requires you to work from a place of serving your dream client. You are not doing something to someone. You are doing something for someone and with someone. That something has to benefit them.

In human relationships, fast is slow and slow is fast. Trying to go fast and get what you want when you want it betrays your self-orientation, creates friction and resistance, and slows things down. Slowing down, making sure that your dream client has what they need to take the next step with you, speeds things up. It compresses the time it takes you to achieve certain outcomes because it eliminates friction and resistance.

Your job is to create so much value for your client during each and every interaction that it is all but impossible to say no to the next step. By creating greater value during every interaction, you are creating a preference for you and what you sell. The more other-oriented you are, the easier it is for your dream client to move forward with you.

Who wouldn't want someone on their team who could help them initiate change and produce better results? This is who you have to be, and knowing how to trade value and control this process is how you help make change.

You have an other-oriented philosophy, a framework for controlling the process, and a strong command of what value you trade for each commitment you need. The next best step for us to take together here is to dive straight into the Commitment for Time. Doing this will immediately help you schedule more appointments with more of your dream clients. What do you look like over the next thirty minutes?

Chapter 4

THE COMMITMENT FOR TIME

SALES ORGANIZATIONS ARE USUALLY HYPERFOCUSED ON CLOSING deals. Sales managers work hard to forecast which deals will close during the current quarter, and constantly ask their salespeople about their deals, focusing almost exclusively on those that are about to close. As a result, deals that are early in the sales process are virtually ignored, even though that's the time when coaching can make a big difference. It's as if the close, or the Commitment to Decide, is the most difficult commitment to gain. But in truth, the most difficult and critical commitment is the Commitment for Time, for without it, you have no opportunities at all.

THE MOST DIFFICULT COMMITMENT TO GAIN

Why is this first commitment so difficult to gain? There are three reasons that come immediately to mind.

First, your prospective client probably already has a relationship with someone who sells what you sell—someone who has a track record of creating value for them and may be considered a strategic partner. So meeting with you may seem like a waste of time.

Second, they probably have a very limited amount of time.

Companies have gotten leaner and leaner in recent decades, and your prospective clients are being asked to do more and produce better results with fewer resources. Time is the only nonrenewable finite resource any of us have, which makes it the most expensive commodity on earth. So potential clients will need a very compelling reason to agree to give you some of their precious time.

Third, your prospective client has probably had disappointing experiences with other salespeople who were unprepared and wasted time. Or they may have been so focused on pitching their products and companies that they offered no value in exchange for time. As a result, your prospect may reject your request for time, thinking you'll do the same. Unfair as it may be, you end up paying for the sins of the salespeople who came before you.

EVEN IF YOU HAVE THE PERFECT SOLUTION...

There is a great cartoon that shows a medieval king in full armor sitting on a horse in the middle of an active battlefield. Arrows fly, castles burn, and a soldier up in a turret dumps hot oil on the enemy directly beneath him. Right in front of the king stands a modern salesperson who's just unpacked his latest product, a brand-new twenty-first-century machine gun—obviously exactly what the king needs to obliterate the enemy. But the king just gives the guy a contemptuous look and announces, "I don't have time to see some crazy salesperson. I have a battle to fight!"

Unfortunately, many of your prospective clients resemble this king. They think they're too busy to meet with you, even if you have exactly what they need to solve their problems. One of your major challenges, then, will be securing the time it takes to show them how you can help!

HOW NOT TO ASK FOR TIME

First and foremost, don't ask for time by e-mail. This one mistake will starve you of opportunities and keep you from reaching your goals. E-mail is an asynchronous form of communication; the exchange of ideas doesn't happen at the same time. You send a message, and sometime later your prospective client responds to that message—or, more likely, doesn't. There is no chance for you to engage with the prospect, resolve her concerns, or explain the benefits she'll get by giving you her time. And it's extremely easy to reject your request. All she has to do is delete your e-mail. None of the suggestions here for gaining the Commitment for Time will work through e-mail. Selling depends on conversations about the future and value creation, conversations that will help to secure the commitments that produce the results your prospective client needs. No such conversations can take place via e-mail.

The phone is a far better medium for asking for commitments. Because it is synchronous, it eliminates the gap in time and allows you to ask for a commitment and respond to the prospective client's answer in real time. It also provides you with the opportunity to elicit and resolve concerns.

It's true, of course, that occasionally someone will hang up on you. But it's a lot less likely than having your e-mail deleted, the digital version of being hung up on. If you like e-mail, it may be because you prefer that form of having your request rejected than you do actually hearing the prospect say no, and then having to ask again.

Now that we've established that e-mail is definitely off the table, let's move on and take a look at surefire ways to get that all-important first meeting with a prospective client.

SIX STEPS TO SECURING THE COMMITMENT FOR TIME

There are six steps you can take to ensure that you get the time you need to see a client, discuss their needs, and offer something of value. These steps should be taken in order and *none* of them should be skipped.

Step One: Ask Early and *Only* for Time

Most likely you will reach out to a prospective client the first time via the phone. And when you do, you must introduce yourself, mention your company, and ask the prospect for the Commitment for Time. Do this as early in the conversation as possible. For example, you might say, "I am calling today to ask you for a twenty-minute meeting to share with you four big ideas that you are going to have to deal with over the next eighteen months. What do you look like Thursday for a twenty-minute executive briefing?"

Don't try to do a lot of value creating before you ask for the appointment. Your dream client hasn't yet agreed to engage in that conversation with you. That value is going to be created during the meeting, as you promised in your request. Similarly, don't try to do discovery work during a call to request a commitment for time. After all, when you start asking questions to uncover your dream client's "pain," you increase the likelihood that they'll disengage with you. The only outcome you should seek during this first interaction is a commitment for time.

Step Two: Expect and Prepare for a No

No matter what you say during your first interaction with a prospective client, when you ask for the Commitment for Time you can expect them to say no. Don't be thrown off. The no is reflexive and has nothing to do with you or your request. As I explained earlier, it may be because your prospective client is already happy with their current provider. Or they've had bad experiences with other salespeople. Or they're so pressed for time they can't keep up with their workload, let alone carve out time to see a salesperson who is unlikely to create value for them.

So consider the first no to your request for the Commitment for Time as a freebie: Every salesperson gets that no. You'll have to earn the next couple of nos by resolving their concerns and asking again. And you'll most certainly have to earn a yes.

Here's an insider's tip: There are only a handful of reasons a prospective client can use to reject your request. And once you know them, you can develop the ability to resolve these concerns, moving you that much closer to a yes. (See "Common Reasons That Prospective Clients Will Refuse to Meet with You" later in the chapter.)

Step Three: Promise Value Without a Pitch

One of the keys to obtaining a meeting *now* is to offer value to the prospective client with no further obligation, including *not* having to listen to you pitch your company and your solution. Perhaps you can offer some new insight into their business that will help them produce better results. Or you may have knowledge that your prospective client will find useful, making you the kind of person worth knowing. Remember, one of your long-term goals is to become a trusted advisor. And that means you must be able to dispense advice. Demonstrate to your prospective client, right up front, that you have insight into their problems and are willing to offer valuable advice, whether or not they decide to take the next step with you.

It's this combination of the promise of value without that pitch that makes it easier for your dream client to agree to a meeting. It will also differentiate you from your competitors, many of whom are still promising nothing more than "introducing themselves and their company."

Step Four: Ask Again

You already know that no matter how terrific your ask for the Commitment for Time may be, you are going to be rejected the first time around, and probably the second as well. But don't be dejected. Remember, it's your prospective client's duty to protect their time. If they say yes to every salesperson who requests an appointment, they won't have time to do anything else. They have to be discerning and try to eliminate time wasters. So expect to be refused. Then continue with the next steps in the process.

A word of caution here: This isn't a battle of wills. You are trying to develop a relationship, not alienate the person with whom you are trying to develop that relationship. If you ask more than three times, you will have crossed over from resolving concerns and asking again to being argumentative. Remember, you are playing the long game, and it is better to preserve the relationship by trying again later.

Step Five: Lower the Commitment Level

A major obstacle to securing the Commitment for Time is the prospective client's fear that they won't be able to get rid of you. They're afraid that you'll overstay your welcome and they'll gain nothing from this considerable investment of time. Here's how you overcome that fear: Lower the commitment level by asking for just a twenty-minute meeting. Most people can afford to take twenty minutes out of their day, and you yourself have just agreed to the end point. Now the prospective client can relax a little bit, knowing that if you turn out to be a time waster, they have an out. In return for a very small investment of time, you deliver massive value in terms of ideas and solutions. It's a big ROI that may prove to be irresistible: little time to gain massive value.

Step Six: Promise Not to Waste Their Time

Since you understand that your prospective client is afraid you'll stay too long and waste their time, you've wisely lowered their commitment level. But you'll also need to assure them that you will not waste their time. You might say something like, "I promise, I only need twenty minutes and I won't waste one minute of your time."

This is crucial. Your prospective client has probably met with scores of salespeople who were time wasters, people who lacked the necessary preparation, focus, and business acumen to be true value creators. You need to demonstrate that *you* are different. And you can do that just by limiting the amount of time you request and promising not to waste a single minute. Do this, and you're showing them that you understand and acknowledge the fact that their time is a valuable commodity. You've also named and addressed one of their most pressing concerns (even if they haven't revealed it) and let them know that you will always respect it.

When you show up for the meeting, don't waste that time. Remind your prospective client of your agenda, let them know what you hope the next steps will be, and begin sharing the value-creating information you promised. Don't start by looking around the room and trying to make a personal connection. Don't start by asking the same questions that every salesperson before you has asked, like, "How long have you been here?" or "If you could change one thing about our industry, what would it be?"

ASKING FOR THE COMMITMENT FOR TIME: AN EXAMPLE

Now let's see what it might sound like when we actually ask for the Commitment for Time, using all six steps in order. Here's the kind of approach I usually take:

> Hi, my name is Anthony Iannarino and I am the business development leader at Transformation, Inc. We help companies improve employee engagement, increase retention, and generate greater results with their existing team. I am calling you to ask you for a twenty-minute meet-and-greet where I can share with you the five trends that are stopping good teams from producing the results they are capable of. Whether or not you ever do business with us, you'll ask some different questions after you see these trends, and you'll likely make some different decisions. What do you look like later this week for a twenty-minute executive briefing?

As you can see, I asked for the Commitment for Time in my initial pitch to the prospect, I offered value without asking for anything in return, and I lowered the commitment level by asking for twenty minutes.

You might be surprised that I didn't begin with, "Hello. How are you?" You might think that I didn't give the person time to engage with me. You probably think I should have tried to connect with the prospect on a personal level. You can't believe I didn't ask how the person was doing or if this was a good time to speak.

Don't worry about any of this. If you use this approach, you will get a response. It may be a question like, "Who are you? What do you want to share with me?" And that's great because it will open the door for you to explain. Or, more likely, you'll get a refusal to your request for time. And you'll be well prepared to handle it.

COMMON REASONS THAT PROSPECTIVE CLIENTS WILL REFUSE TO MEET WITH YOU

You already know that your request for the Commitment for Time is going to be refused, probably several times. The good news is there are a finite number of refusals out there, and once you understand the pattern of an appropriate response, you'll be able to resolve most concerns and schedule more appointments than most salespeople. Here are some of the most common ones, plus responses you can use to resolve the concerns.

"I Am Happy with My Current Partner"

A reason frequently used by prospective clients when refusing to meet with new salespeople is, "We are happy with who we're using now," or something similar. Then they might add, "We don't want to waste your time." You, knowing that your one and only goal at the moment is to gain the Commitment for Time, might respond like this:

> Excellent. I understand you have a provider you are happy with now. Almost everyone I call already has someone providing services similar to ours. I'm not asking you to change anything, including your partner. But I would like to share some ideas with you during a twenty-minute meet-and-greet. Should your situation ever change in the future, you will know me and you'll know how we think about the big challenges your industry is facing now. If your situation changes, I want to be the first person you think of. What do you look like Thursday afternoon?

Even if we never work together, these ideas are going to change some of the decisions you make over the next twelve to eighteen months.

You have lowered the commitment level and offered the prospective client value in exchange for time, value that he retains even if you never do business together. Here's another example of a good response:

> I expected that you'd have a strategic partner helping you. In many of the companies that we work with, we act as a supplement for the work that they do. There are a couple of areas where you may find that you need us in the future, and it never hurts to know someone should you need something different then. What do you look like for a twenty-minute meeting late Wednesday morning? I promise I will be respectful of your relationship, and I'll share these ideas with you just so you have some new options in how you might approach your business, even if we never work together.

The truth is, your confidence will go a long way toward encouraging your dream client to say yes to your request for an appointment. If you don't sound like you are certain about your ability to create the value you promise, your dream client is going to sense that incongruity and refuse to make the commitment.

Be sure to ask again for the appointment after resolving the concern. You don't want to solve the problem and then just sit back and admire your work, that will only invite another objection or concern. Stay focused on your outcome and ask again.

"I Don't Have Time"

A lack of time is a very real concern for many people, especially those who have great responsibilities. Such people are often overcommitted, with more work to do than anyone could handle in two lifetimes. You are now asking for another chunk of their time, exactly what they don't have. Here's a tip: Most busy people are booked up at least a week in advance, so asking for time a couple of weeks in the future may make it easier for your prospective client to say yes. So you might say:

> I imagined you would be very busy. Most of our clients are, and we're always working on ways to help them reclaim some of their time. What do you look like two weeks out? I'll keep the meeting to twenty minutes, and I'll leave you with a copy of the executive briefing I'll be sharing with you.

Most likely you'll get another refusal based on the lack of time. Your prospective client might ask you to call back in a quarter or at the beginning of the following year. But you need to set an appointment now, not later. So be polite and professional, but ask again for an appointment. This is critical. Most salespeople give up and give in at this point. But if you want a meeting, you'll have to persist.

You can say, "I understand that you're very busy, but I am totally convinced that the ideas I would share with you during a twenty-minute meeting would pay dividends for you over the next twelve to eighteen months, whether you buy from me or not. You tell me when twenty minutes works, and I'll be there."

As always, you must promise value that's greater than the value of the time you're requesting. You need to be so convinced that you can create value for the prospect that you feel comfortable asking again, directly, for the meeting you need.

"Mail Me Some Information"

Here's another common way of getting rid of you: "Why don't you mail me your information? Then, if I'm interested, I'll give you a call."

Here's a news flash for you: No one really wants you to mail your information. Unless a prospective client happens to be an insomniac, he's probably not going to peruse your four-color brochure. It won't create any real value for him, nor will it forge a relationship between him and you. Mail doesn't serve you or your prospective client well. E-mail, as I said earlier, is even worse.

As with other kinds of refusals, you'll have to ask again. You can say something like:

> I'm sorry. The meeting I'm asking for really has nothing to do with me, my company, or my solutions. At this point, it's really not important that you know us and what we do. It's more important that we share a few ideas that can help you make some different choices in the future, no matter who you work with. There's nothing that I could mail you that would have as much impact as the ideas I can share with you in a twenty-minute conversation. I promise to limit it to twenty minutes. You tell me what works for you this week and I'm there.

A DIFFERENT APPROACH

To make this approach work, you are going to need to have the insights and ideas that you can trade as value for the Commitment for Time. If you don't do something different, you are going to look and sound like every salesperson who has come before you, increasing the odds you get a no.

THE COMMITMENT FOR TIME

When you think about it, many of the commitments you are asking for through the sales process include a commitment for time. You need to ensure you have the value proposition that equals the Commitment for Time that you are asking for at all stages of the sales process.

COMMIT TO TAKE ACTION

Review this script and answer the questions that follow.

Salesperson: Good morning, Jane. This is Todd Smith with XYZ. I am calling you today to ask you for a twenty-minute meet-and-greet conversation where I can share with you the four big trends in information technology that are likely to impact your business in the next twelve to eighteen months, and the questions you and your team are going to want to explore. What do you look like this Thursday afternoon for a twenty-minute executive briefing?

Prospective client: Thank you, Todd. We already have a supplier, and we're not interested in changing.

Salesperson: I expected as much. I am not asking you to make any decision about changing suppliers. What I would like to do is share this briefing with you. I promise it's going to change some of the decisions you make over the next year and a half, whether we ever work together or not. I'll be respectful of your existing relationship, and if you ever need anything in the future, I want to be the first person you think of. I promise it's twenty minutes, and I'll leave you with the slide deck so you can share it with your team. What works for you in the next couple of weeks? I won't waste your time.

Questions:
1. What value can you offer your dream client that makes it worth their while to give you some of their time?

---

2. What questions should your dream client be asking themselves and their team about their future?
3. What concerns does your dream client have about giving you their time?
4. What have you done during sales calls that was not a good use of your dream client's time?

Thanks for sharing your time with me. I'd love to continue this conversation and share some ideas of other commitments you need to obtain and how to gain them. Can we turn the page together and explore a little deeper?

Chapter 5

THE COMMITMENT
TO EXPLORE

THE COMMITMENT TO EXPLORE IS THE PROSPECTIVE CLIENT'S
agreement to consider that a change might be necessary in order to get
better results. This may sound fairly easy—it's just agreeing to think
about what a change might look like. But most people are highly resistant to change, especially if they think things are working pretty well
as they are. You'll need to convince them that change can be a good
thing, then explore the ways that you might work together to make
these changes.

EXPECT TO ENCOUNTER RESISTANCE

Resistance from a prospective client is a given. Nobody is a "lie down,"
and everybody is trying to protect their positions, ruffle as few feathers
as possible, and keep from making mistakes, especially expensive ones.
So you'll run into all kinds of reasons why prospective clients won't
want to buy what you're selling. And it begins with the denial that they
need anything at all.

"I'm Not Dissatisfied"

If you're like most people in sales, you were probably trained to make your first meeting about "discovery." That is, you would ask questions designed to uncover the prospect's dissatisfaction with the status quo, so you could attempt to solve his problems. If you weren't able to identify the dissatisfaction, you were told, you wouldn't be leaving that meeting with anything resembling an opportunity. No dissatisfaction, no change, no deal. The flaw in this logic is the assumption that the prospect will be dissatisfied when you find him. Most likely *you* were the one who initiated this meeting—since ready-to-buy leads are as rare as unicorns—so the prospect won't necessarily believe he has a compelling problem. And he certainly won't be harboring high hopes that you'll offer some much-needed solutions.

In a similar vein, it's also likely that a prospective client will be deeply entrenched in the status quo. If she believed she had a compelling reason to change, she would have done so already, or at least be working on it. Instead of changing, she has probably found ways to work around her challenges. She may even be telling herself that everything's okay—not perfect, but okay. For most people, sticking with the old ways of doing things is a much more comfortable approach than venturing into the unknown. And as long as she does this, she won't have to struggle to convince other people in her organization that they too need to make unwelcome changes.

"The Problem Is Really Very Simple" (Not!)

Whenever a prospect begins to engage with a stranger (that's you in this case), there will always be a certain amount of resistance to discussing the "real" issues. They don't really know you, and there hasn't been enough time to create much in the way of trust. They will undoubtedly want to protect their ego and avoid being judged, thought poorly of, or embarrassed. During exploration, you're trying to find out where the failures lie, what isn't working, and what's wrong with the current situation. You want to dig deep and find the root causes of their problems or challenges. This can be threatening, so don't be surprised when your prospective client clams up or is more willing to discuss the problem at hand than what lies deeper.

But if you're going to be of any real help, you and your prospective client *must* deal with the source of the problem rather than the presenting problem. Here's an example: One of my clients is troubled by a very high employee turnover and wants a better, more consistent workforce. He presents the problem as if it's due to the poor quality of people they've been hiring, but that's not the root cause. The root cause involves a number of different factors, including their onboarding process, how they support new hires as they learn their jobs, and what they do (or don't do) to make them feel safe in their new environment. Because my client believes it is simply the quality of the individuals the company has hired and not problems from within, he bounces from partner to partner. Only when I am able to show him that many of the people his company dismisses end up working very successfully in the business across the street is he willing to address the real problem and find real solutions.

Your task, then, is to get a prospective client to dig deep enough during discovery to get to the root cause of the presenting problem. It may mean having uncomfortable conversations. But if you want to be a trusted advisor, you have to be willing to "go there" and explore—to identify and address the real issues, so you can get the commitments that allow you to solve the problems.

DISCOVERY ISN'T JUST ABOUT "THEM"

Your first meeting with a prospective client is a discovery meeting, but you're not the only one who's trying to figure out the situation. While you're trying to learn about their challenges, they're trying to work out the source of their concern and what they might do differently. And they're also trying to decide what kind of partner you'll make. Are you filled with ideas that can help them solve difficult challenges? Can you be trusted to help them make changes? Do you really know what you're talking about? Don't forget that everything you say will contribute to the overall impression you're making!

"WHAT'S KEEPING YOU UP AT NIGHT?" IS THE WRONG QUESTION

No doubt your client has already agreed to meetings with salespeople who showed up, tried desperately to develop rapport, and then asked a series of clunky questions designed to get them to reveal the areas where they have problems. Very few of these meetings turned into anything more, and your prospective client felt the salesperson wasted their time.

In the last chapter, we promised to show up prepared to provide value outside of selling the client our solution. We promised to share our insights about issues that are impacting our dream client's business—or that soon will be. This is a different form of discovery, and it's extremely effective because it focuses on setting the stage to explore change.

You are going to be defined by your approach to discovery. And employing the standard approach, which is often some variation of asking the client, "What's keeping you up at night?" is likely to leave you defined as a time waster.

I have no idea how old that question is, but I've never personally asked it. It sounds like something you would say if you had no idea what to say. For many reasons, it is a low-value-creating question. Imagine you are your dream client. A salesperson walks into your office and says, "What's keeping you up at night?"

You think, "What? *You* don't have any ideas about what I should be concerned with? You don't have some theory about the areas that someone in my position might be challenged with, or where I might be struggling with results? Don't you have any clients you are already helping? Haven't you learned anything from helping them with whatever it is you sell?"

Congratulations! You're dealing with a time waster!

Since you asked for the meeting, *you* need to trade real value for that meeting. You must be prepared to do deeper-level discovery, one that considers the new reality that your dream client isn't already compelled to change. You must know what *should* be compelling them to change as a starting point for discovery.

MISTAKEN ASSUMPTIONS

The reason so many salespeople do poor discovery is because they assume their dream client *already is unhappy* with their current situation—so unhappy that a few standard questions will uncover enough dissatisfaction to create an opportunity.

I recently received a call from a salesperson who was trying to obtain my business. He started by telling me that he wanted to work with me and my company, and that he could do better work than my current partner. He asked, "What do you think your current provider could do better?" Unfortunately for him, I didn't have a list of complaints about the company doing this work for me. I told him, "They're doing a really good job, and we have a long relationship. I am not going to change right now, but I'll keep you in mind should I need something." With no compelling reason for me to change, the salesperson went to the only thing he knew, saying, "I am certain I can save you some money." The little money I might have saved is meaningless in the big scheme of things; the quality of the work is important enough to pay more.

This is the problems with assumptions. By assuming I would already be compelled to change, that I knew what I should be compelled by, and that my current relationship wasn't important, he failed to even engage me. Had he started by sharing with me the current state of the industry, what new results were possible, and how he could improve upon what was being done, he might have done better.

This salesperson didn't ask me to explore change, and he didn't provide me with a vision of what was possible. What should he have done? He might have given me an update on the state of technology in the business and how it could benefit me and my business. He could have shown me the gap between what I think is possible and what is actually possible. He could have created a gap between my results and my competitors' results by showing me what other people are doing.

Let's look at some of the common mistaken assumptions salespeople make.

Assuming There's a Compelling Case for Change

If your prospective client already believes that he has a compelling reason to change, he'll either be working on that change or have already made the change. So walking into his office and assuming he'll be ready to make some major alterations is a mistake.

That being said, it's also true that nobody is completely happy with the way things are going. So you can safely assume that your prospect is experiencing a certain amount of dissonance; he just may not be unhappy enough to change yet. He knows that something isn't right and things aren't working well enough, but the dissonance he's experiencing hasn't quite morphed into a compelling reason to change.

The goal of your first meeting, then, should be to explore this dissonance and define it as a problem worth solving.

Here's an example. I have a friend in the insurance business. The dream clients he calls on tend to be experiencing some level of dissonance and know that something is wrong. They're paying the lower management fees that his competitors promise, but they're spending more than they expected. They're also not getting the results they were promised; their insurance claims aren't being managed well.

When my friend visits these clients, he explains that although they pay lower management fees, their insurance providers' contracts allow them to collect money for managing all the ancillary services they provide, fees that are way beyond the profit they forgo by offering a lower management fee. The result is that they underinvest in the management of the actual claims and focus on the ancillary stuff. That's good for them, but not so good for their clients.

By explaining their dissonance to his dream clients, my friend turns a conversation about how their industry works into a compelling reason to change—namely, that they aren't being served by his competitors' business model and are overpaying for results they aren't really getting. As soon as they understand how the different models work, he creates a case for change, and he almost always wins their business.

Assuming Clients Already Know Why They Should Change

Don't ever expect a prospective client to tell *you* why they need to change. Answering the question "Why should I change now?" is your responsibility. And only when you've answered it to their satisfaction can you engage in an exploration of change and the creation of worthwhile opportunities.

You may be waiting for your prospect to tell you what they need because you think your prospective client knows their business better than you do. And when it comes to the minute details of *their* business, they undoubtedly know more than you. But your prospect is most likely a heads-down kind of person, working hard at running their business. And that means they might not have a bird's-eye view of what's going on in their industry, or what others may be doing differently. You, however, do have that knowledge, and that's what makes you extremely valuable.

So you share information your dream client doesn't have about their business and what's going on industry-wide, and share the experiences of others just like them, who are doing what they do. They want and need to know more about their world. Do whatever you can to acquire the business acumen you need to be relevant (or go get you some "chops," as I like to say!), then be prepared to share it.

Assuming That Status Quo *Isn't* King

If you're like most salespeople, you probably underestimate how difficult it is to effect change. Yet few competitors are more difficult to beat, and none have more allies, than the status quo.

Your prospective client has been doing things a certain way for a long time and he's found work-arounds for whatever isn't working as well as it might. Within his company, others are busy protecting their turf, and many may have adopted a "silo mentality" in which people in the same organization don't share information, so they operate more or less independently. Change isn't something they engage in easily, quickly, or without a great deal of thought.

This is what you're up against. Now you must lead the exploration of change by helping your client with their discoveries about their business, as well as their discoveries about you. Then you must build a case showing that their results can be vastly improved by eliminating or replacing whatever is impeding progress. You must explore the ways you might work together to make these changes. And you must be clear about the risks that will continue to grow as long as the status quo remains in place. Finally, you must acknowledge the two constants that are involved in every new venture: Everyone wants things to be better than they are, and change is difficult. But that doesn't mean it can't happen.

"WHY SHOULD YOU CHANGE?" IS THE RIGHT QUESTION

If things can't be better than they are right now, then there is no reason to change. To commit to dealing with a sure-to-be messy and disruptive change initiative, the client must believe that the payoff will be far greater than the pain. The starting point of discovery is building that compelling case for change.

This means that you need to know *all* the reasons your dream client should change. You need to know what better results are available to them, and what's preventing them from obtaining those results. You also have to explain how the risks will continue to grow as long as your dream client remains committed to the status quo.

Everyone wants things to be better than they are, but change is difficult—sometimes very difficult. It's up to you to instigate that change by building the case that things can be better than they are. You need to help your prospective client explore the reasons they need to change so you can gain the next commitment, the Commitment to Change.

The value you create for your clients doesn't come from asking them what's keeping them up at night. It comes from telling them what *should* be keeping them up at night. And to know the answer to that question, you need business acumen. You need to know things that your dream client doesn't know. Salespeople aren't valuable when there is information parity between them and their prospective clients. You're valuable because you know things they don't. You have different knowledge and different experience.

Answering the "Why Should You Change?" Question

You already know how to make a standard discovery call. You know how to put together a series of questions that allow you to uncover the problems, issues, challenges, and opportunities that might lead your dream client to change—including changing suppliers.

No doubt you've been taught to wait to present until after you've done your discovery work. Waiting to present until after you know what your prospective client wants or needs provides you with the chance to connect your solution to those needs.

All good advice. Sometimes. But what if they're not already compelled to change, not fully aware of why they should change, and deeply mired in the status quo?

When you encounter such a client, which is most of the time, you need a different approach. You need to begin exploring change by sharing your insights and your point of view about your prospective client's business, their risks, and their opportunities. Remember, you promised to create value during this first meeting by sharing some big ideas, ideas compelling enough to be worth your dream client's time whether or not they ever did business with you. The way to open that conversation is to provide your dream client with the five big trends that deserve their attention.

Unless you have an enlightened marketing department that will provide you with this type of content, you are going to have to do your homework. And that begins with considering issues such as:

- *What are the primary challenges your dream clients face that your solution would solve for them?* This should be an easy question for you to answer; you already know what problems you solve.
- *What are the root causes of each of those problems?* The presenting problem and the root cause of that problem are different. In Chapter 14 of *The Only Sales Guide You'll Ever Need,* we called this "the ground truth." Why do so many of your prospective clients have this problem?
- *What are the economic, technological, cultural, political, or scientific trends that are causing the problem or challenge, or creating an opportunity?* Pick the five most compelling to build your case for change. And be sure to choose the trends that bring real consequences when unaddressed. Does it have to be five trends? Would four, or even seven, be better? The number doesn't matter, but you want a powerful list that can be delivered in around twenty minutes.

The important outcome here is for you to present your view of your client's business, their threats, their opportunities, and some insight about other choices available to them. In other words, make it clear to them why they should change—and why you are the one to help them do so.

SOME QUESTIONS YOU MIGHT ASK YOURSELF

If you come to the early meeting prepared, your dream client will pepper you with questions throughout your presentation of "Five Big Trends

Worth Your Attention," or whatever you call your explanation of what *should* be keeping them up at night. They will also share with you their thoughts about how these trends are impacting them and their business. This means you are engaging at a higher level than you would have been had you simply asked, "What's keeping you up at night?" and the other standard discovery questions.

Your presentation has engaged your client's attention, and they're going to want to know more. They'll want to know what other people are doing to address these issues, and they'll want to know what you are doing to help your clients. This may not be the approach to discovery you've been taught, but sharing your opinion about what your dream client needs to change, and why, is powerful. Armed with knowledge and a strong opinion, you are relevant to them—very relevant.

You can also close your presentation with a list of "Some Questions You Might Be Asking Yourself Right Now." Questions like, "How is this trend impacting our business now, and what should we do in response to it?" Or, "How can a business like ours take advantage of this techno-logical change?" You create value by creating the case for change, not by sharing your company history. Questions like these are more com-pelling than anything about your company.

What's Next? Surfacing Areas for Further Exploration

After this first meeting, you need to ask for another commitment. This commitment will most likely be another discovery meeting, and your contact may want to invite other people to listen and explore. You may initiate the ask by saying, "It sounds as if there are two or three areas here worth exploring. What do you look like next week at this same time for a meeting? I'll bring some ideas about what we see working, and you can invite anyone from your team who can give us their ideas and feedback."

No tie-downs. No clunky closing technique. Just natural language and a promise to create future value.

You might hear, "We're not quite ready to address this now."

You can reply: "I wouldn't expect you to be. This isn't easy stuff. I understand that you aren't ready to make a decision now, but I would like to meet again to help frame this up so that should you decide to do something in the future, you'll have some ideas about what might work. I'll bring some of our best ideas to share with you, knowing it is going to be some time before you're ready to do anything. We can do this in forty-five minutes. You say when over the next two weeks, and I'll be here."

Depending on who you are meeting with and their role, you might also say: "I know you aren't ready to address this now, but I'd love to share with you some ideas about what you might consider when deciding to change. Can I meet with a few members of your operations team to better understand their needs? After I do that, I'll report back to you with what I learned and some ideas about what might work for you. Is there someone who can help me understand this challenge at the runway level?"

Doing a good job in your first meeting makes it easier to gain the commitment for a second meeting. If you have trouble getting that second meeting, you probably didn't create enough value in the first meeting to deserve another. If you fail to obtain this commitment, ask for a do-over. Call your prospective client back and say, "I don't think I did a good job explaining what we should do next and why you would want to have that meeting. Can I start over?" You will find that doing this immediately after leaving a client meeting is easier than getting them on the telephone or getting a response to your e-mail.

What Kind of Partner Would You Make?

Are you a great salesperson?

Do you know exactly why your prospective client should change? If you don't, and if you can't help them explore the consequences of the status quo, you aren't creating value for them at this stage of their process.

- Can you name the four or five trends that are going to cause your prospective clients problems now or in the near future? If not, you don't have the advice they need now.
- Can you share your experiences helping other people in similar situations with their challenges? If not, you don't have the insights and experience that would indicate that you're the right partner.
- Do you have the advice your clients need? Do you know things they don't know? Have you helped other people produce better results? Can they trust you? Are you going to help lead this change, or will you sell them and disappear?

Early meetings with a prospective client are where you create a preference for you, your company, and your solution. If you show up with a slide deck, determined to tell your dream client about your company by showing them your company's history, your organizational chart, and all the logos of the well-recognized brands you serve, you aren't going to create a preference. You're going to create an aversion.

So go to the early meetings prepared to demonstrate that you can answer yes to all of the questions above—in other words, that you would be a very valuable partner for them.

COMMIT TO TAKE ACTION

Review these scripts and answer the questions that follow.

EXPLORE I

Salesperson: Thanks for letting me share this briefing with you, Jane. It sounds like two of these big trends are already impacting your business. I have a couple of additional resources I can share with you around both of these challenges. What do you look like late next week? I'll bring you the additional resources we discussed, and I'll share a couple of ideas of things that other people are doing to make improvements in those areas.

Prospective client: Can you also send me your slide deck and those questions?

Salesperson: Absolutely. I'll send those as soon as I get back to my office. What does Wednesday afternoon look like for you?

Prospective client: I could do something after three p.m.

EXPLORE II

Salesperson: These two topics were interesting to you last time we met. Tell me more about what you're thinking right now.

Prospective client: The technological shift you shared with me last time is becoming a real problem. We've known for a long time that we are falling behind here, but we've been so busy that no one has given this the time or attention it needs. We're really not sure what we should be doing.

Salesperson: Well, we have some strong opinions here. We believe the right solution is to make two changes. The first one is an equipment change. The second one is a process change. Honestly, the

technological change is easy. The process change is always more difficult, but you can't get the best results without making it. We've
tried.

Prospective client: We're not so good at changing process here.

Salesperson: Who is? Can I show you some of the choices you might
make and what is possible?

Prospective client: Sure.

Questions:
1. What are the most common root causes of your prospective
   client's challenges?
2. What are the forces behind those challenges? What external
   and internal forces cause them?
3. What do you need to teach your prospect about their challenges?
4. What do you do to create a preference for you and your solution at this stage?

We've covered a lot of ground, and it seems as though you are eager
to continue. If you don't need anything else at this point, can I ask you
to move to the next chapter with me?

Chapter 6

THE COMMITMENT TO CHANGE

LET'S SAY YOU'VE GONE ALL THE WAY THROUGH YOUR DISCOV-
ery process, come up with a great solution, and presented to the key
stakeholders. Then three months go by, and even though you've had a
number of nice conversations, nothing has moved. Has the opportunity been lost?

Or how about this: One of your contacts at the prospective client's
company really wants to make serious changes. You've had a few good
discovery meetings, and she has continually agreed that she needs to
do something soon. She promises to get back to you, but you're still
waiting. Is this deal dead in the water, or simply a "stalled" opportunity?

Unfortunately, neither of these can be categorized as true opportunities because both lack the all-important Commitment to Change.
Until you've secured your prospect's Commitment to Change, all you
have is a lead. Nothing more. And nothing you've discussed—problems,
challenges, needs, desires, budgetary constraints, or the value you can
create—means a thing. For a real opportunity to exist, your prospective client must agree that they have a compelling reason to change and
that they want a better future state. Securing the Commitment to
Change is the most important part of the entire sales process.

THE WORST THING CAN BE NOT CHANGING

Change is difficult. It's messy and it can be political. It often involves disrupting the business. Those within a company who try to promote change often upset the powers that be, and they suffer the consequences for having done so. Resistance to change becomes a form of self-protection. I have one client who decided against making a change because to do so, in his words, "would be political suicide." That's a strong statement, but if you've been in sales for any time, I'm sure you understand the sentiment behind it.

In truth, as difficult as change may be, the greater danger often lies in not changing. Refusal to change can result in the obsolescence, irrelevance, or complete disappearance of a business or even an entire industry. You may remember that for decades Kodak was a top manufacturer of film and cameras. When one of its own employees invented the digital camera in 1975, the senior management didn't understand its relevance and refused to market this new technology for fear of damaging their profitable film business. They didn't want to make the change. In fact, they feared this kind of change. As a result, other companies developed their own versions of the digital camera and Kodak was forced into bankruptcy.

Entire industries are suffering these days because they aren't keeping up with the deep disruptions and fast-paced change caused by new technology. Taxi companies, for example, could have created a service like Uber, but they didn't. Great hotel chains could have founded Airbnb, but it never occurred to them. News organizations could have come up with Facebook and Twitter, but they never imagined there was any reason to change. This is what happens when companies stop innovating, ignore technology, and stop changing—and it's the *real* danger you must help your clients face.

HOW TO SECURE THE COMMITMENT TO CHANGE

You can get your prospective client thinking about the need for change by asking some powerful questions. You might shy away from them because you're afraid of offending them by "going there." You may think that you'll put the deal at risk if you bring up the difficult issues involving change. But what really puts the deal at risk is not having these conversations. The ability to have these conversations is what will transform you from "salesperson" to "trusted advisor" and "strategic partner."

You may also be reluctant to find out how far your prospective client is from making a commitment to change. You may not want to face the bad news, but you need to find out where the process stands. If you look at your pipeline report right now, you will find so-called opportunities that are past their time. These prospects haven't made the commitment to take the next step, even though you believe they will buy eventually. Some of them will continue to meet with you, and you'll probably have many nice conversations. But unless these conversations address the need for change, they will not end with a commitment to change, and you'll wind up with nothing.

I happened to be visiting a certain company when an executive leader was reviewing what was in the pipeline for its frontline sales managers. As each pipeline report was projected onto a screen, a sales manager stood up and explained to the group how his deals added up to enough opportunities to reach his goal.

The charts I saw on the screen each had a column that indicated how many days an assigned salesperson had been pursuing the "opportunity." I was stunned to see that one had actually been in the pipeline 1,741 days! I had to use the calculator on my smartphone to figure out that this "opportunity" was just a few months shy of its fifth birthday. If it were a child, it would be starting kindergarten!

There was no way this company's average sales cycle was anywhere near five years; it was more like nine months. And yet there were dozens of opportunities that far exceeded the nine-month mark; many of them were over one thousand days old.

I also noticed that most of the expected closing dates were March 31, June 30, September 30, and December 31. These dates indicate the end of a quarter. No one's prospective client wants to change to a new partner on the last day of the quarter. Most likely, the sales manager had asked the salesperson, "Do you think you can close the deal this quarter?" The salesperson had replied yes, then set the expected closing date at the end of the quarter so as to have as much time as possible to try to wrap it up. This meant that the sales manager was allowing his salespeople to keep nonopportunities in the pipeline, which kept them from doing the real work necessary for the creation of true opportunities: prospecting.

I was curious to find out how many real opportunities the company had in the pipeline. After eliminating all the "opportunities" that had been in their current stage more than twice as long as the average deal won during the past couple of years, I found it was less than a third of the original figure! That's because most of what was listed on the charts weren't opportunities. They were leads—and some of them were very old leads.

You don't want to be in this situation, so you need to ask the powerful and difficult questions that you might fear. That is the only way you're going to move the sales process along.

Questions to Ask

You and your prospective client have explored the changes and improvements that could solve their problems and bring them closer to their desired future. Now it's time to find out if they're really ready to make a change. Ask if you're on the right track and they're ready to attend to the problems you've been discussing by saying something like:

> Are the problems we've been discussing the right ones for you and your team to work on right now? Or do you have others that are more pressing?

In other words, is this something they're ready to move on right now? Or ever? Hopefully, they'll say, "Yes. Now is the right time. This is important." But you might hear instead that they're not interested in addressing the problems now or in the future. And that's good to know. If you're totally on the wrong track, it's much better to find out sooner rather than later.

Whatever their reason, it will be worthwhile for you to know and understand it. So ask something like:

> Can you share with me what is preventing you from moving forward now?

You may also hear that your prospective client has a more pressing issue to deal with before they can commit to making a change. That's vital information for you as well. Once you learn their priorities, you have possibilities. You can try to change those priorities by demonstrating the importance of addressing the problems you discussed first. Or you can set a date to discuss these problems again once they have addressed their current priority. If your prospect truly isn't going to make the change for another six months, you need to know that and deal with it. It doesn't mean that you aren't going to win the deal. It just means that you aren't going to win it on your current timeline.

You'll have clients who can't make any real changes at the moment because they can't disrupt their business in peak season. Others will lack the personnel necessary to make changes. Some may need to wait until an additional person is brought on to their team so that person can participate in the decision to change and help decide whom to bring on as a partner.

If you want to be a trusted advisor, you must value relationships more than transactions. If you try to force a change right now, you are placing too much value on the transaction. But if you work to gain commitments that allow you to play the long game, you'll preserve the relationship. And remember, you are playing for lifetime clients, not a quick win. You might say something like:

> I understand completely. Can you tell me what your timeline looks like? Perhaps we can use the time between now and then to do some of the necessary work, should you decide to do something different.

You might be able to use the time to analyze their data so as to better understand their current situation, and to further develop their solution. There may be a reason and opportunity to meet with your prospective client's team to customize the solution to fit their specific needs. You might be able to begin having the meetings that allow you to develop your solution during the weeks or months before your dream client can agree to change. What you want is a commitment to do something that moves you closer to winning their business. Selling requires you to exercise your resourcefulness. Be creative, and do whatever you can to keep the process moving forward.

Now let's say everything turns out great and your dream client agrees that this is the right time for them and their team to work on these problems. You may be tempted to move forward without asking any more questions. But your next question should be something like:

Will others who are impacted by the changes you make understand the need for them? If so, do they have the ability to deal with a change like what we are looking at here?

It's a lot better to know up front if others in the organization are going to resist this new vision of the future, rather than finding out later that the status quo killed your deal. If you know resistance is coming, you might be able to convince those who are against you that the change is in their best interests.

Again, let's say all systems are go. Your wrap-up should be something like:

Great. We have more work to do, but what's your best idea of a target date for rollout [completion, execution, delivery, etc.]? I want to provide you with milestones as we continue this conversation.

The target date is not your date; it's the client's date. When your sales manager asks you if that date is real, you can confidently say, "Absolutely!" You will need medical care standing by to revive your sales manager when you tell him that the client suggested this as the right date to change!

THE TURNING POINT

Securing the Commitment to Change is one of the things that separates professionals from the pack. The ability to "go there" and have difficult, meaningful conversations with a prospective client is what moves a deal along and transforms a "salesperson" into a "trusted advisor" and "partner." Amateurs avoid the difficult conversations about change because they don't want to be uncomfortable and are afraid of their prospective clients' reactions. They think these conversations may put their deals at risk. But what really puts a deal at risk is *not* having these conversations.

HOW TO TELL IT'S NOT AN OPPORTUNITY

There are three telling clues that will let you know that you aren't looking at an opportunity; you're simply chasing a lead. They are when the commitment process has halted, the client has no compelling reason to change, and the client has no vision of the future. Let's take a closer look at each one.

The Commitment Process Has Halted

One of the best ways to discern whether you're working on a real opportunity is by assessing your prospective client's commitments. If he has not yet agreed to the Commitment to Change, you can no longer call the deal you are working on an opportunity or even a "stalled" opportunity. It's something less than that, more like "a qualified, interested lead." I'm not suggesting that you stop working to win your prospective client. But if you do intend to continue, you'll have to gain another commitment. The more time that passes and the more meetings you have without your prospect making that commitment, the less likely it is that you'll successfully close the deal—ever.

If you are truly pursuing an opportunity, your prospective client will be aware that he is engaged in the process of change. Think of it this way: If I called the first three prospective clients in your pipeline and told them you believe you will be signing a contract with them by the close date you have in your CRM, would they be surprised? Would you be worried about my making that call, believing it would damage your relationship? If the answer to either of these questions is yes, you may be pursuing leads, not opportunities.

No Compelling Reason to Change

The products or services you sell may be far superior to those your prospective client is using now. You may be infinitely better at producing the outcomes you've promised than are your competitors. The contacts you call on may be wildly impressed when you explain what you do, how you do it, and how it will benefit them. Yet if a prospect doesn't really believe they have a compelling reason to change, she won't. And you won't make the sale.

One of the great challenges you'll face as a salesperson is that your prospective clients don't want to change. They've learned to live with their problems and believe "that's just the way things are." Even though they're not completely happy, they've been managing long enough that the problem has lost its power to force a change. Would they like things to be better? Absolutely. Are they compelled to make a change? Not so much. This means that it will be your job to help your dream clients become unhappy.

"Wait," you may be saying. "I thought my job was to make them happy, help produce better results, and move them toward a better future!" Yes, those things are important. But you can only make these things happen once your prospects have decided that change is necessary. Unfortunately, they don't usually do this on their own. So unless you help them find a compelling reason to change, they will probably just keep doing what they've always done. And you will *not* be looking at an opportunity.

No Vision of the Future

Sometimes a prospective client doesn't feel compelled to change because they don't have a vision of the better future that is available to them. As I mentioned in the last chapter, they may have limited exposure to other companies or the industry itself and not be aware of what's new and relevant. If they can't visualize the better outcome that you're promising them, the sales process ends here. Therefore, it's your job to paint that picture, to make a better outcome not only visible in their mind's eye but attainable. You can help them get there because you're constantly seeing, hearing about, and learning about new discoveries, theories, facts, and bits of information that can do much to boost your prospect's efficiency, output, and success. You must use that information to provide them with a vision.

Fortunately, this shouldn't be too difficult. Your prospect is probably worried about what he doesn't know. He wants you to help him see around the corners. He wants to know the risks he may be exposed to. He wants to know about the opportunities available to him, and what's possible. So paint the picture of a compelling future and keep the opportunity in play.

YOU CREATE OPPORTUNITIES FOR CHANGE

Many of the companies you call on won't believe they can have it any better than they have it now. Having changed partners before, only to end up with the same problems, they will have given up on improving. This is why the Commitment to Change is crucial.

If you are going to be a rainmaker, you have to make it rain, which means that you create new opportunities. You are the catalyst for change. If there is no vision, you have to help create one. You are going to need to be collaborative in designing and developing that vision, but you are also going to have to share what is possible when your dream client isn't aware of the better outcomes available to them.

COMMIT TO TAKE ACTION

. . . .

Review this script and answer the questions that follow.

Salesperson: It seems like these challenges are preventing you from producing the results you need. Does it make sense for you and the business to work on these challenges now?

Prospective client: Yes, it does. We need to do better here.

Salesperson: How is the rest of your business going to respond to the idea of doing something different here?

Prospective client: Well, some people on my team are going to be excited by doing something different. Some of the other areas that are going to be affected by a change aren't going to want to do something different now.

Salesperson: Can you share with me what's going to prevent them from wanting to do something different?

Prospective client: They're comfortable with the way they do things now. They're going to think it's more work, and that it isn't worth the effort.

Salesperson: Is it still worth working on this, even if we are going to have to work to persuade them to come along with us?

Prospective client: I think it is. We need to do something different here.

Salesperson: Can I share an idea with you? Let's get together and do what we can to build the right solution here, and we'll collaborate to

---

try to give them something they can support. I can come back next week at this time. Who else should join us in this meeting to talk through what you really need here, and what is going to work?

Prospective client: That works. I'll need to bring two people from my team.

Questions:
1. What are the compelling reasons your dream client should change now?
2. Why are some of the opportunities in your pipeline stalled?
3. What commitment do you need to gain to move these opportunities forward?

As you have no doubt noticed, this book is collaborative. You are looking at scripts to come up with your own powerful language choices. You are also answering some really tough questions. In the next chapter, we'll look at how you can collaborate with your dream client and increase your chances of winning their business. Can I recommend that you turn the page so we can make you unstoppable?

Chapter 7

THE COMMITMENT
TO COLLABORATE

ONE MAJOR REASON THAT SALES ORGANIZATIONS LOSE OP-
portunities is that they believe their solutions will work for any prospective client. They don't tailor their products, services, or results to
the prospect's specific needs. In short, because they neglect to collaborate with their prospective clients, they lose a deal they very well might
have won.

Collaboration with a prospective client is essential. Always invite
them to help you make decisions about how to produce their desired
outcomes. Don't assume that whatever you're selling will automatically
solve their problems. Always customize your solutions and outcomes
to ensure they fit the prospect's needs. If you don't or you can't, you'll
lose the deal to someone who does provide them with what they need.

CHANGING "YOURS" TO "OURS"

"Just send us your proposal and pricing," says your dream client. "Give
us your very best ideas. Let's see what you've got."

The problem with presenting your solution is that it is "yours." It
belongs to you. It doesn't belong to your dream client. You might be

absolutely head over heels in love with your solution. You might believe it is better than any of your competitors' and anything your prospective client has ever seen. While it is critically important that you believe in what you sell, it's even more important that your dream client believes your solution is something they can say yes to.

How do you make sure that you give your dream client a solution they can say yes to? By collaborating with them on designing that solution. You invite your dream client into the process of designing the solution, and you transform "your solution" into "our solution."

One client my team was calling on had a serious turnover issue. We wanted to help them solve this issue, but we recognized early on that we wouldn't be able to resolve it alone. Their managers and supervisors would have to change what they were doing with the new people being placed in their departments. To come up with a solution that they could embrace, we met with their leadership team to share our ideas and then asked for a meeting to collaborate with their team. We set the stage by sharing our view of the reasons why their turnover was as bad as it was; then their leader asked what they could change to improve it. Instead of immediately presenting our ideas, we encouraged them to come up with a list of a half dozen things, including changes to their onboarding process and providing new employees with a mentor or coach. We then added a couple of ideas that would support them. This process not only helped us win; it helped us execute later—something I believe would have been impossible had we not collaborated.

Truth be told, we could have made the same recommendations without having this meeting. The outcome, however, would have been far different. It was their participation in deciding what the right solution was going to look like that allowed them to support it.

When the stakeholders you are working with inside your dream client's accounts have designed the solution with you, their commitment to that solution is stronger. They have greater ownership. They have skin in the game. They're committed to the solution because they're getting what they want. When all of these things are true, you have allies who are willing to defend the solution you recommend because they feel it's theirs.

MAKING ADJUSTMENTS

You have ideas about what your dream client needs to do to address what is compelling them to change and to deliver the better future they need. Your ideas are solid. They're likely tried, true, and tested. But they're yours. As good as they are, you increase your chances of winning your dream client's business when you improve them. And who knows how to make the improvements that transform your solution from "good" to "perfect"? The people who work inside your dream client's company.

Here's an example. In one of my businesses, we provide on-site management of the employees we provide. These on-site managers are there to manage the employee onboarding process, employee relations, and all administrative work, and they act as a liaison between the client and our company.

One client we worked with loved the idea, but needed something different. Instead of an on-site manager with the normal job duties, they needed someone to actually supervise the work of the employees we provided them. As they explained their needs, it became clear that our solution wouldn't work for them. It wasn't going to provide them what they really needed. What they needed was outside of what was customary, and it wasn't something we provided. For our client, this was going to be a deal breaker. So we collaborated and built a solution that created a new role. This was something that we had never provided, and it required us to fundamentally change our service offering. It was difficult for some on our team to deliver, but it made it easy for the client to say yes to our proposal. In the end, it not only helped to win the business and generate the outcome the client needed, but it also gave us a new offering.

When something you are going to do isn't going to work for your dream client, you have to make adjustments, like the new role we created. If what you are proposing isn't going to work as well as they need it to, you are giving your prospective client a solution to which they have to say no.

Let's talk about making adjustments. Sometimes you will need to make adjustments to your solution. You'll have to do something different, maybe even something that you haven't done before. The new role that we created wasn't too popular in our own company. It meant that some of the work we needed the on-site individual to do would have to be done by someone else. Selling it internally was more difficult than selling the client. If you are going to sell successfully, you are going to have to sell inside your own company as well as you sell outside. You have to make the case to change your process, invest more resources, or develop a new program. Everything you are learning in this book can easily be applied inside your own company. In fact, if you collaborate with your dream client to make adjustments, it will more than likely be necessary that you collaborate inside your own company.

The changes required to produce a better outcome may also need to come from your dream client's side. They might have to change the way they do things now. They might need to make adjustments of their own, and quite possibly adjustments they don't want to make. Persuading your dream client's key stakeholders to do things differently isn't easy either—and that's why we call it selling. In the case above, we had to ask our client to change the way we priced our solution to accommodate their needs.

COLLABORATIVE CONVERSATIONS

Collaboration can be defined as two or more parties working together to generate new ideas, capture feedback from all involved, and then make adjustments. In a true collaboration, all parties work together to produce and optimize the outcomes. Forming a collaboration with your prospective client will greatly increase your chances of making a sale. The best solutions always come from a combination of ideas. And since you'll gain a great deal of insight into what your prospective client is seeking, you should be able to come up with a proposal they will almost certainly agree to.

But first you need to gain the Commitment to Collaborate. The language you use to gain it might sound like this:

> I'd like to share some ideas with you and your team, then get your feedback as to what might work and what we need to change to make this work for you. Who do you think we should include, and what's the best day to do that next week?

Note that not only are you asking your prospect to collaborate, you're also asking for a commitment for time, something you will do repeatedly throughout the sales process.

A collaboration might consist of your prospect and you, or of your prospect, their team, and you. In general, anyone who is going to be involved in the final decision making should be part of the collaboration if possible. For simplicity's sake, let's say you've formed a collaboration with the prospective client only.

It will be up to you to get the ball rolling. Start by giving your prospective client something to respond to, as in, "Here are some ideas that I think might work." Then follow with a preliminary rundown of ideas or solutions that could help them generate better results. This rundown isn't the same thing as your final presentation. You're just batting around ideas. It's not formal, you may not have any visual aids, and since you're still exploring, it may not even resemble your final proposal. Once you've finished, ask your prospective client for feedback and invite them to suggest some of their own ideas. Only then can you and your client start making adjustments.

After you've presented, a prospect who isn't used to collaborating may simply say, "It looks great!" and not give any additional input. But I would caution you against accepting this as the truth. They may be intimidated, or may not realize that you'd be willing to go in a direction you haven't mentioned. So be sure to encourage the prospective client to speak their mind. Ask directly, "Which part of this might not work for you, and how would you change it?" You don't want to wind up with a no at the end of the sales process because you didn't realize that your solution was off track.

Hopefully, your prospect will be frank and clear about the changes they'd like to see, and you'll need to try to incorporate those changes. But you must also understand the reasoning behind their desired changes. Say something like, "I understand you want to make this particular change, which may be a very good idea. But just for my own edification, can you tell me why you need this done this way? What problems do you have when you do it another way?" Once you understand the thinking, you can push it a little further by asking, "If we make the changes you've described, would that work for you?"

You may have to make multiple recommendations and changes before you find something that works. If you're dealing with just one person, assume you haven't spoken to all who will be impacted by the decision to change, and be aware of the fact that some of these people may resist your solution because their needs weren't considered. Try your best to arrange collaborative meetings that involve more stakeholders.

Now let's say that, either due to the collaborative process or sheer luck, your solution seems perfect to all involved and no changes are deemed necessary. Still, you'll need to ask, "What else would you need to make this exactly right for you?" You want to cover all your bases and collect all the information you need to make any adjustments necessary to get you to yes.

THE KEY TO A LONG-TERM RELATIONSHIP

The need to collaborate doesn't disappear once you present your perfectly tailored solution, or even once your prospect signs the contract that magically transforms him into a paying client. It continues for the life of the relationship and will pay endless dividends. Collaboration is the single best route to identifying new opportunities, creating new value, solving problems, and improving the level of service you give to your clients. Your conversations with clients that are centered around "What do we do next?" and "How do we make this even better?" will transform you from vendor or supplier to strategic partner. And they will lay the foundation for a relationship built on teamwork and cooperation rather than conflict. In the future, whenever problems crop up, you and the client will have a process for resolving those issues already in place. You'll both know how to come up with the most effective solutions to any challenge. The level of trust between you will continue to grow. And you will have earned the right to create and win the next opportunity.

COMMIT TO TAKE ACTION

Review this script and answer the questions that follow.

Salesperson: Here are some of the areas we need to discuss together today. This will let us build a program that gets you the results you need now, and that better positions you in the future to add additional capabilities. What do you think the right solution looks like?

Prospective client: We are going to have to have a solution that allows us to continue to do the three things that we are doing now. We can't lose those capabilities.

Salesperson: I've got that. We need to make sure you can still do what you are doing now in these three areas.

Stakeholder 1: Whatever we do, it's going to have to be integrated into our current system. There is no way we can go back and forth between two systems. We have to have a single access point.

Salesperson: Integration is a big deal. That makes total sense to me. We can do that. We'll make sure whatever we come up with is integrated into your current system.

Stakeholder 2: Are we going to have a single point of contact? Who are we going to be working with on a day-to-day basis?

Salesperson: That's not customary, because we use a team-based approach. Can you share with me why this is important to you?

Stakeholder 2: If our team has to work with different people and bring them up to speed all the time, they're going to get frustrated. They don't want to go over the same ground all the time.

Salesperson: You'd actually have three people assigned to you, but they would all know your business, and they work very closely together. Would that work for you?

Prospective client: I am not sure. It sounds good to have more than one person, but I am not sure it's the same as having one person who really knows us.

Salesperson: Okay. Would it be okay if I showed you how we work, and you can decide if it works for you? If it doesn't, could we create a role for a team lead, so we don't lose access to the subject matter experts we need to make this work?

Stakeholder 2: We'll look at it.

Questions:

1. Whom do you need to meet with to collaborate and customize your solution?
2. When you have won a deal in the past and had trouble executing, who were the people on your client's side who didn't get what they needed? What needed to change?
3. What customizations or changes have you had to make to win deals that might be useful in future deals? Where did each of those changes come from?

Who else on your team really needs to read this book right now? Can you invite them to join us here, so you can work on some of these ideas together?

Chapter 8

THE COMMITMENT TO BUILD CONSENSUS

COLLABORATION IS WORKING WITH SOMEONE TO PRODUCE OR create something. Consensus is an opinion or position reached by a group as a whole. These two commitments work together. To collaborate, you need people to work together. To build consensus, you need people to agree to go in a certain direction. Thus, you may need a consensus to agree to collaborate. And after you've collaborated on a solution, you need a consensus to agree that this is the solution the group wants to implement.

Today, in most large corporations, consensus is king. The people with titles and roles indicating they are "decision makers" no longer want to take action unilaterally. In fact, it's likely that unless forced to do so by extreme circumstances or emergencies, they won't. Leaders today don't want to make a decision that they have to ram down their people's throats, and they don't want to create problems by not allowing the people who are going to be impacted by a decision to help shape that decision. So while you may have been taught that you need to find and work with "the authority," likely someone with a C-level title, it's now more likely that the power to decide has been distributed among multiple stakeholders, all of whom have a say in the change initiative. This means that you don't need "the" decision maker. You need a consensus.

WHO'S GOT THE POWER?

I once made a presentation to fourteen people at a prospective client's company. At the conclusion, after I had answered three or four questions, it suddenly occurred to me that most of the fourteen people had the power to say no to the sale and kill it. But no one person had the power to say yes and make it happen. There was no single authority.

During the question-and-answer period, I tried to figure out who might have enough authority to at least initiate change. What I noticed was that many of the questions weren't being directed to me. Instead, they were directed to the supply chain manager, the human resources manager, and one technical person. As soon as any of these people answered a question, they would immediately direct a question to one of the other two.

I took a chance and decided to try to set a meeting with each of the three individually. I met with the supply chain manager, who then recommended that I meet with the human resources manager. After that meeting, I got the green light to work with the company. (As it turned out, the technical person wasn't essential to the decision-making process.) Obviously, a consensus was needed at this company before a decision could be made. But it didn't involve the entire group. I had to figure out who had the power and who didn't.

WHY LEADERS LIKE GETTING A CONSENSUS

To understand why decisions are being made by consensus, you need to understand what motivates the company leaders to choose this method. It's pretty simple: Company leaders want "buy-in" on major decisions—that is, they want assurance from those affected by the decision that they will participate in the change initiative from the start. If the leader doesn't have buy-in, those who actually do the work will be less committed. And they won't necessarily put in the time, resources, and energy needed to produce the outcome. Some may simply resist the change effort, while others may actively work to ensure that it fails. If, on the other hand, those who must execute the change are allowed to participate in a consensus, they will be more committed to the decision. And the leader can hold them accountable for making it work.

This is true even for those who don't want the change and didn't get what they wanted. Consensus doesn't require unanimity—only that everyone has the chance to participate, be heard, share concerns, collaborate, mitigate the challenges, and vote. Some will have to stand down in the name of what's best for the organization. But all will still be accountable for the execution of the change. Once the group agrees to the change initiative, all members will be on the hook to make it work.

FEARS THAT GET IN THE WAY OF CONSENSUS

Reaching a consensus when making major decisions may be a good thing for businesses. But it makes selling more difficult for you because more people are involved. You'll need to identify and gain access to these individuals, and possibly to the stakeholder groups they represent. Unfortunately, the identities of these individuals may not be something your prospective client is willing to supply, for a number of reasons, including fear of losing control, fear of stirring up the natives, and fear of extending the process.

Fear of Losing Control

Your prospective client may be afraid that if she allows you access to the other stakeholders, the opportunity the two of you are trying to build will be changed in ways that don't serve her. In other words, she's afraid that she'll lose power and the ability to direct the action.

She may think that keeping the opportunity under wraps is a way of protecting it. But if the other stakeholders aren't involved early on, there is a risk that their needs and concerns won't be adequately addressed by your solution. You and the prospect need these stakeholders to support the opportunity. It will be much easier to gain a consensus if you involve them in the process of creating the solution, giving them not only power but ownership.

Fear of Stirring Up the Natives

Your prospective client may be afraid that bringing the stakeholders into the discussion will stir up a hornet's nest of resistance. Throughout any company, support for the status quo can be deep and wide. If your solution is implemented, certain people are going to be forced to accept changes, and many of them won't like it. Resistance to these changes can come from an entire department or even from sectors of the company that have very little to do with the solution you sell. For example, you might sell payroll services, yet you find you're getting resistance from the information technology department because they don't like your security requirements. Or the purchasing department is balking because the stakeholders didn't allow them to lead the buying process. Or perhaps a company insider has a strong relationship with your competitor that they're willing and able to defend. For reasons like these, your prospective client may prefer that you put off interacting with other stakeholders, at least for a while.

Fear of a Longer Process

Your prospect may not want you to involve other stakeholders because she's afraid it will drag out the process. Bringing in additional people means setting up more meetings, having more conversations, dealing with more disagreements, and just plain spending more time. She may also fear that certain people who oppose her idea may try to "run out the clock"—that is, stall the process until the proposal to change simply runs out of steam. I've seen it happen a number of times, even when the change was necessary.

These fears are real. But your prospect is mistaken in believing that skipping or putting off consensus building is a better idea than embracing and engaging it. In reality, if these meetings don't happen, those who are not included often work to oppose the change. They stall decisions. Excluding people who are eventually going to get their say only causes greater resistance because no one had the courtesy and professionalism to include them.

In human relationships, fast is slow and slow is fast. If you want to speed up the time it takes you to create an opportunity, win that opportunity, and deliver results to your client, slow down. Do what is necessary to get all the commitments you need leading up to the Commitment to Decide. If you want to slow down the entire sales process, just try skipping over some of the commitments you need, especially the Commitment to Build Consensus. Many—if not most—salespeople skip this commitment, and that is why their deals die. Many of their clients encourage them to skip this commitment.

WITHOUT CONSENSUS, NO DEAL

The real danger you have to address is the danger of a "no decision," which is the decision not to make a decision. A "no decision" produces the same result for you as a no when you ask for the Commitment to Decide. All you do by avoiding the tough work of building consensus is to move that decision forward in time. You lose the opportunity earlier rather than later.

Much of the time spent calling on a single stakeholder—even one whom you believe to be the decision maker—ends with a decision to do nothing. This is true even when the single decision maker you are working with needs the outcomes you sell, and even when she may be able to say yes without anyone else's consent. More and more, decision makers refuse to go it alone and decide.

If you look at the deals you are working on now, in how many of them are you working with a single stakeholder? If what you sell is strategic, comes with a good bit of risk, and requires a relatively large investment, being single-threaded is a mistake. The decision to buy will not be made by a single person. Not knowing who is really making the decision to change is a mistake, and it puts your deals at risk.

Look back over your notes from the last few meetings you've had with your dream clients. How many times did you meet with one stakeholder alone? If there were more people in the room, have you had the necessary conversations with them to be absolutely certain you have their support? If you don't know that you have their support, then your deal is at risk.

HOW TO GAIN THE COMMITMENT TO BUILD CONSENSUS

If you know you are going to need to bring other people into the sales conversations that lead to change, you want to talk about that with your contact very early in your process. You want to gain an agreement that building consensus is going to be necessary, and that you are going to help your prospective client get that consensus. Remember, control the commitments, control the process. Lose control of the process, lose control of the outcome.

This is how you control the process. You preview the commitments you need by sharing your process, and then you work to earn the right to ask for those commitments. When you lose control of the process, bad things happen.

Early in the process, you need to gain the agreement to build a consensus from your prospective client. You might say, "At some point, we're going to need to bring those who will be involved in making this decision into the conversation. Who are we going to need, and when does it make sense to bring them into our discussion?"

There is a lot in this ask. You have presupposed that other people will be involved, that you need them to be involved, and that your prospective client agrees to both of these. Then you return control by asking your prospect when it makes sense to bring other people into the conversation. You hope she will respond with a list of names and a confirmation that the next meeting is the right time to start. But it doesn't always go the way you hope it will.

Let's say she replies, "I am the one who will make this decision. I'd prefer not to have anyone else involved."

If that language doesn't scare the life out of you, it should. You know that you aren't likely to win a deal with only a single stakeholder weighing in on the decision. Being single-threaded is too risky, and it's more likely you will lose to the status quo than you will find your way to a positive outcome. Is she telling the truth? She might be, but it's not likely, even in smaller deals. More often than not there will be multiple stakeholders.

You can respond with something like, "I understand you have concerns about bringing other people into this conversation. Can I share something with you?" Wait for her to say yes, indicating her desire to learn more, before continuing with, "It's been my experience that when we don't involve anyone else in this process, later on they either work to oppose what we're trying to do or make it really hard to execute. Is there a way we can identify the people who will be involved in decision making, and build the support we need without losing control of what we're doing?"

Or you might say something like, "Who can we bring in now who will be supportive and help us build support from the other people we need?"

Listen, none of this is easy—for you or your prospect. Your job is to do whatever is necessary to serve her, even when you bump up against resistance. You may not get what you need on the first attempt. If your prospective client tells you that she alone will make the decision, or she will make it for her team, you are going to need to use skillful means to ask again and uncover who else is going to be instrumental to a decision to move forward. You might try another approach by asking, "Who would support this decision and might help us with the insights we need to make sure everyone gets what they want?"

If your prospect gives an indication that she knows where resistance might come from, you can be very direct. Ask her, "Who do you think is going to resist what we decide here?"

Some stakeholders will oppose a change because of an internal political squabble, or because it doesn't serve their long-term goals. But more often than not, they have very real concerns. It will be your job to work through this process.

For example, let's say your prospect confides that the IT department would probably resist the change because they already have too much on their plate. You can reply, "Is there a way we can help them get additional resources so they'll support us?"

By helping remove obstacles to change, you will increase your prospective client's preference for working with you. And why not? You are valuable because you know how to make change. You are valuable because you can work with them to help them build consensus and initiate change inside their own organization.

The Commitment to Build Consensus isn't a particularly easy commitment to obtain. But once you do, you will establish yourself as a valuable and effective partner—one who knows how to bring about change. Not many people can make that claim.

Remember: The Commitments to Collaborate and to Build Consensus work together. To collaborate, you need the commitment to bring people into the process. To build consensus, you have to collaborate to design something that is going to work. That's why it's important to be thinking of creating consensus even as you are working on collaboration, and vice versa.

COMMIT TO TAKE ACTION

Reviews these scripts and answer the questions that follow.

CONSENSUS I

Salesperson: In order to make this solution work, we're going to need to bring in your X department and get their buy-in. When does it make sense to involve them in this process?

Prospective client: Never. You have no idea how difficult they are to deal with sometimes.

Salesperson: Ha ha! I can imagine. Well, we can't avoid them forever. Eventually, they're going to know we are up to something, and the longer we go without letting them in on the process, the more prickly they're going to be. Who is the one person in that area who will give us a fair hearing and explore these ideas with us?

Prospective client: Jim. He's the only reasonable person in the whole department.

Stakeholder 1: Yes, Jim is the right person. He already wants to make changes there.

Salesperson: Can we invite Jim to join us?

CONSENSUS II

Salesperson: Thanks for joining us, Jim. What we are discussing would mean making some changes in your area. We would never do that without including you and your team in this process. Can you share with me a little about how what we are doing is going to impact your team?

Jim: Well, it's going to make things much more difficult for us, even if it makes things better for the company. It means we are going to have to change the way we do things now, and it's likely going to take more time and effort than we can afford right now.

Salesperson: Can you help me understand how it's going to take you more time and more effort to make the kind of change we're discussing?

Jim: Our project board is full right now. Adding this project means we would have to stop working on another project. All of the projects we are working on are important, and they all have deadlines we are struggling to meet now. So tackling this would push something else back.

Salesperson: Are there projects that aren't as important, with deadlines we might be able to move back, if we could explain why it is important to do?

Jim: If there actually was something we could push back, we could reduce the massive overtime we're working now. Pushing a project back just to add new work would frustrate my team.

Prospective client: What if you had more people on your team, Jim? What if we found you the resources?

Salesperson: Where would we find those people?

Prospective client: We could pull a few people from another project outside of Jim's department, and we could get an outside vendor we use to work on this project.

Jim: If we brought in an outside vendor, I'd use them on another project before I'd use them on this one. I already have a skills gap that I am struggling with now.

Salesperson: Hypothetically, if we could get you a couple of people from another team, and bring in an outside vendor to shore up your team where it really needs help, would that help you? Would you need anything else?

Jim: I'd still need more time.

Salesperson (to prospective client): Can we work around Jim's timelines?

Prospective client: Of course we'd like to go sooner, but we'll have to do what we can.

Salesperson: Okay. Let me put together a plan and milestones, and we'll look at that together early next week. Does that work?

Questions:
1. Who is normally impacted by a decision to buy your product, service, or solution?
2. Who tends to resist your solution after it has been delivered? What negative consequences typically cause their resistance?

3. What trade-offs do you normally need to make so that people in different departments can agree to the changes that come with your solution?
4. How many of the deals you are currently working on include only one stakeholder on the client's side?

Getting the most from this book is going to require that you match your investment of money with an equal investment of time. It's more time than you are used to spending on a single book, but it is the only way to transform your results in commitment gaining. Does it make sense for you to make this investment and generate better results now?

Chapter 9

THE COMMITMENT TO INVEST

BEFORE YOU CAN MOVE FORWARD, YOU NEED TO GET YOUR prospective client to agree to invest the time, energy, and capital necessary to produce the desired results. And that means it's time to discuss price—right now—if you haven't already. "What?" I can hear you saying. "Isn't that a little premature? Shouldn't I wait until I deliver my proposal?" You might think that if you start talking price too early in the game, and yours is higher than your competitors', you'll scare off prospective clients before you show that you can create real value for them.

While it's true that a lot of salespeople reveal the price only when they submit a proposal (and have been doing it this way for a long time), here's what's generally true: If you withhold the necessary conversations about price until the end, your price will be compared to your competitors' and you'll be asked to discount. But if what you sell carries a higher price because it's better, there's no reason for you to compete this way. Once your company has made the strategic decision to differentiate its offering by creating greater value, you're going to be quoting a higher price than your competitors. And you aren't supposed to be competing—or winning—on price. You're competing and winning on value. This means you'll need to find out sooner rather than later whether your client believes that price trumps value. Because if the answer is yes, you're probably wasting your time.

Some salespeople who offer high-end products or services actually lead with their higher price as an indication of the greater value they're offering, and to test the water. They know that if the prospect balks at the price, it's best to discover this early and move on. That's because there's no point in creating an opportunity, building a compelling vision of the future, and gaining consensus from the necessary stakeholders, only to have the deal fall through at the end when your prospective client is surprised by the numbers. Not only is it possible that they'll be taken aback by the price, they may also think you were hiding it all along and wonder if you're trying to take advantage of them. In short, while it may be tempting to leave price out of the equation as long as possible, it won't serve you or your company or help "preserve" a deal.

DON'T WASTE YOUR TIME

Prospective clients who will ultimately waste your time include those who don't understand your value proposition, can't afford to make the investment, have business strategies that conflict with yours, or simply don't want to spend the money because they believe things are already "good enough." There are some prospects who will never value what you do, how you do it, or the greater outcomes you provide. Even when you prove you are demonstrably better, when you're selling the Mercedes-Benz of your category, they won't be willing to pay for it. For example, companies like Walmart that compete on the basis of price want to get the lowest price from their suppliers. To them, it won't matter how much better your product, service, or solution may be. So you might as well find out early and then steer clear.

In short, even though you may be afraid of losing the opportunity, don't leave the price conversation until the last minute. Moving it up in the process will increase your odds of winning the deal at a higher price. Take the plunge. If you can't secure the Commitment to Invest, it's time to move on to other opportunities.

The time to determine what the right investment needs to be is *before* you ask for the Commitment to Decide.

THE DANGER OF UNDERINVESTING

Most of the time, generating better results requires making a bigger investment. Naturally, most people would prefer to get the former without coming up with the latter. (Who doesn't dream about getting something that's not only better and faster but cheaper too?) And some people actually believe they can operate this way. You've probably had prospective clients who bounce around between suppliers, always looking to pay a little less. Then they're surprised and perplexed when their results are disappointing. They don't seem to understand that things that are "better" and "faster" are almost never "cheaper." After experiencing several disappointments, buying a more expensive product or service sounds dangerous. They're skeptical of your promises to generate excellent results and afraid to spend money on what they think could be another letdown. They simply aren't convinced they'll receive the additional value you are promising.

It's your job to help a prospective client see that the greater danger he faces—a danger far greater than increasing the size of his investment—is *underinvesting*. If your competitors could produce the outcomes he needs at a lower price, they would already be producing those results. If price is his only consideration, he will constantly jump from one provider to another on the "great race to the bottom," where the "winner" reaps thin margins, problem clients, and a miserable business.

I've worked in staffing my entire adult life. Some of my clients have mission statements describing their people as their greatest resource, yet they invest as little as possible in them. I have seen prospects rush to pay a lower price only to incur higher overall costs because of the way certain services are billed. I've seen some companies lose their clients while their strategies come apart at the seams due to a lack of investment, which translates to paying too little to attract the talent they need.

And what I've learned is this: If a company wants to get more, it need to spend more. There's no such thing as better, faster, *and* cheaper.

I've also learned to lead with price. I begin with, "We can help you get the outcomes you need, but our price is going to be higher than what you are paying now."

This statement serves your prospective client by telling him the truth about what he needs to invest. It also makes you a trusted advisor, the kind of person who is going to tell the truth about what he needs to do to produce the outcomes he desires.

BUILDING VALUE AND JUSTIFYING YOUR DELTA

You dream client can't have better, faster, and cheaper. No one can. The laws of the universe simply forbid it. If your dream client wants better, they need to invest more. If they want faster, they need to invest more. If they want high caring, high trust, and high value, they need to invest more. A greater investment in any outcome makes it more likely that those outcomes will be obtained. A smaller investment almost always means reduced outcomes with more problems.

What if your dream client wants cheaper? Then they have to pay the higher cost that comes with the cheaper solution. "Wait," you say. "How does a lower price equal higher costs?" When your dream client pays a lower price, they are giving up better and faster. They are pulling money out of their solution, making less money available to produce those outcomes. When has it ever made sense to invest less money in an attempt to produce greater outcomes? When someone wants a lower price, that is their real outcome.

Think of how many times you've purchased something cheap only to be disappointed with your experience. How many times have you underinvested in what you really needed only to spend more money later? Don't you wish somebody would have cared enough to tell you the truth and help you invest a little more to prevent paying a much higher cost later?

Your dream client can't have better, faster, and cheaper, and you can't give it to them. You aren't ever going to be the person people count on for help if all you can do is lower the investment and put the outcomes they need at risk. That's what order takers do.

Do Not Fear Your Price

If your price is higher than your competitors', you must be able to "justify your delta," or explain the difference between yours and theirs and still make the prospective client feel it's worth it. It can be tricky, but you can do it. You say, "Our price is going to be a little more than our competitors', and it's going to be a little more than what you are paying now. Can I share with you how investing a little more will ensure that you produce the outcomes you need and lower your overall costs?"

This is offense, rather than defense. You aren't bracing for complaints about price. Instead, you are about to teach your prospective client how to think about the investment she needs to make and how that investment will drive the outcomes. And you'll provide your prospect with the information she'll need to defend this investment later, when her team asks why they are paying more. Reminding your prospect of the value you have already created for them up to this point is also useful in helping them recognize why your higher price is justified.

There are several reasons why your prospect may benefit from paying more for what you're selling, including:

- Better results
- Your product lasts longer, which means your prospect will need to buy less overall
- Your prospect will get back the hours they would normally spend working around certain challenges
- A better experience

The price is much less than the costs incurred without your product or service. Here is an example of the price versus cost justification. My team and I once won a big account from a company that was often short a few people on their manufacturing lines because of the way they operated. That is, the company would call us at the last minute hoping we could backfill the positions of people who had called in sick or otherwise didn't show up. But by the time they notified us, it was usually too late to get anybody to their facility, so the company would end up shutting down lines and sending people home. Shutting down a line cost them about $5,700 an hour in lost profits, so no matter what price the company was paying us to supply workers, their real costs were $5,700 an hour more when a line was down. We proposed that we send the company two additional people every day as an "insurance policy" against having to shut down lines. And what they paid for that "insurance policy" was far less than the profits that they had been losing a couple of times a week. The company paid more so that we could deliver results that ultimately saved them a bundle.

Investment Comes Before Solutions

You need to make it clear to your prospective client that when she pays a lower price, she is pulling money *out* of the solution, which means less will be available to produce her desired outcomes. This is the exact opposite of what she should do. The investment needs to drive the solution, not the other way around. Your prospect can't expect to stay at the Ritz-Carlton paying Motel 6 rates, own a Mercedes at a Kia's price tag, or eat at a three-star Michelin restaurant for the cost of dinner at McDonald's. The same is true when it comes to purchasing what you're selling. Find out what your prospect can and will invest, and if it's less than the price you're asking, build a solution to match that investment whenever possible. You may have to reduce or eliminate part of what you would normally recommend, and you still might be quoting the highest price. Just be sure you're offering the best possible solution for that investment.

Greater Value Is a Wedge

A lot of salespeople are afraid of their higher price. But a higher price indicates greater value. You and I both use price as a shortcut when we make buying decisions. In one of my workshops, I ask participants what they buy that always has to be sold at the lowest price. They respond with things like "razors" and "gasoline." And, of course, there is always one person who shouts out, "Toilet paper!" But when I ask how many people buy the cheapest toilet paper they can find, everyone laughs and no one raises their hand. Why not? Because we all know that cheaper can't be better. They also don't buy the cheapest coffee, nor do they drive miles out of their way to save a few pennies on gasoline, recognizing the cost of the gas to get to the cheaper station eliminates any savings.

The greater investment you require is actually one of your competitive advantages. It is a wedge that you drive between your prospective client and your competitors: proof that you create greater value. So when you hide the fact that you cost more, you're projecting that you *aren't* really better than your competitors. Buyers will instinctively feel that if what you're selling was worth the price you're asking, you'd have no qualms about discussing that investment. So share your higher price early, and establish yourself as the greatest value and the best solution.

No one considers the salesperson who can pull money out of his program his trusted counsel. The person who tries to sell by taking money out of the equation doesn't have the skills or abilities to generate that level of relationship. That salesperson is just trying to make selling easy instead of being a strategic partner.

The person whom your dream clients look to for advice and counsel is the person who can help them justify a greater investment necessary to produce the better results they need. You need to be the person that can help your client make the right investment.

SHOW ME THE MONEY

If you're going to gain the Commitment to Invest, you need to use the right language. Lay the groundwork by stating that your price is going to be higher. You might say something like, "We are not going to be the cheapest solution. You are going to see other companies with lower prices. Does it make sense for you to invest a little more to produce the results you need, and avoid the problems you're having now?"

Using this language, you tie the investment to the outcome. You are also establishing your dominance as the greatest value.

But let's say you're not yet sure what the prospective client's investment might be. You still need to do more discovery work. You can gain the Commitment to Invest by saying, "Based on our conversations so far, I believe the right solution is going to cost something between X and Y. Does that sound like we're in the ballpark, and would that investment make sense to generate the outcomes you need now?"

Getting this kind of agreement early on will make it easier for you to design the right solution and avoid difficult negotiations later on, because you've already agreed that the investment is tied to the outcomes.

Now let's move on to the next step. You've named your price and are waiting for the inevitable questions, objections, or concerns. There's probably not a prospective client out there who will agree to your price immediately, especially if it is on the high end. So be prepared to hear some or all of the following:

That's More Than We Thought.

This may be a test. Don't overreact and start babbling about discounting your price or asking your manager for permission to do something else. Simply remind your prospect of what she will get in return for her increased investment. You can say something like, "I understand. The reason a lot of the companies we work with aren't getting the results they need is because they are underinvesting. Your present investment isn't getting you the results you need. This one *will* produce those results and eliminate the higher costs you are paying in other ways. Does it make sense to invest a little more in order to get the outcomes we are working on here?"

We Don't Have the Budget.

Everyone has the budget (or they can find it) for what they truly believe they need. You may have to help them find it. You can ask, "What do *we* have to do?" making sure to emphasis the word "we." Remember, you must be your prospective client's partner in finding this money. You may, for example, have to generate an ROI calculation to show her how she is already spending the money she doesn't believe she has by operating in her current fashion.

You might say, "By not making this investment, you'll end right back where you are right now. If this is the right solution for you, as we both believe it is, how do we help you get the budget you need?"

You might also say, "Taking anything out of this solution also reduces the outcomes we are able to generate by reducing the investment in those results. Can we find the budget, or should we look at a different solution?"

If your prospective client truly doesn't have the money or can't access it, you may have to change your solution. If you can give her less and still get her to a better place than she is now, making changes to your solution may make sense.

Your Competitor Has a Lower Price.

Clients *have* to ask for a lower price; it's part of the job. They have a responsibility to their companies to make good decisions with the money they spend. So you are always going to be told your competitor has a lower price. Own up to it immediately by saying, "That's right. They are always cheaper."

You might want to let that one sit right there for a minute. Then follow up with, "They're a good company and a lot of good people work there. We just invest more than they do in generating the results our clients need, and we don't make some of the concessions they make to give their clients a lower price and different outcomes. Our model is different. That's how we generate better outcomes in the areas where you want to make a difference. Would it make sense for you to invest a little more to generate the results you need?"

You might also say, "Is a lower price more important to you than a lower overall cost?" Then explain the difference between price and cost. One young salesperson I know explained it this way: "I am too poor to buy cheap stuff. I have to buy nice shirts and shoes because I can't afford to replace them three times a year."

Once you've gained the Commitment to Invest, you will have made great strides through the sales process and be ready to concentrate wholly on the solution. Just make sure it is something so packed with value for your prospective client that she will find it absolutely irresistible!

COMMIT TO TAKE ACTION

Study this script to plan your own client dialogues and answer the questions that follow.

Salesperson: I've done some preliminary work on the solution, and it looks like the overall solution is going to cost somewhere between $750,000 and $825,000, plus the additional costs of bringing in an outside vendor, the way that we are looking at this now.

Prospective client: Wow! That's more than I expected, and it's more than we have ever paid. Why so much more?

Salesperson: There are a couple of reasons. First, your existing partner had you underinvesting in the outcomes you are trying to get. Their solution is good, but not effective at the volume you are doing now and will be doing as you grow. The reason you have the two bottlenecks in your performance is because you don't have the throughput you need. This investment corrects that. The ROI on the increased throughput on what amounts to $75,000 more is massive. It will double what you can do now. We are also investing more in support and services, so you won't have the maintenance expenses you are

---

experiencing now. The price is higher than you pay now, but the cost is going to be significantly lower.

Prospective client: I understand that doubling throughput is worth investing in, but I am not sure about the ongoing support and maintenance.

Salesperson: The maintenance agreement we are looking at is going to lower your costs by about 30 percent. Our team can do this work at a lower cost than an outside vendor, and it's our solution. Can I show you our analysis?

Last year, you used over two hundred support hours and paid just over $40,000. The same level of support in this package will cost you just under $29,000. Overall, you are going to spend plus or minus $100,000 more than you are spending now. Does it make sense to invest a little more than you are now to double your throughput and eliminate the challenges you are having now?

Prospective client: My team is going to worry about spending more and not getting this kind of improvement.

Salesperson: I understand. If I were in their shoes, I'd want to be certain it was worth the time and effort to make this kind of change before running down this road. Can we get your team together for a preproposal meeting to review the solutions with them and get their feedback? They can share their concerns with us, and we can make modifications to make sure they get what they want.

Prospective client: That makes sense. I want their buy-in before we move forward.

Salesperson: Can we get the operations and information technology teams together for this preproposal meeting?

Prospective client: Some of them. I'll make sure we have a representative from each team.

Questions:

1. What outcomes do your clients fail to produce when they underinvest?
2. In what ways does underinvesting cost your prospective clients more than the difference between what they are doing now and your higher price?
3. What do you do differently that justifies your higher price?
4. Why do you wait to reveal your price at the end of the process? How would moving that conversation up help you keep your prospect from underinvesting?

I know it's late. I know you didn't expect to read this much of this book so fast. If it makes sense, we can plow forward together and learn to gain the Commitment to Review. Or we can pick this up tomorrow? What works best for you?

Chapter 10

THE COMMITMENT TO REVIEW

BY NOW, YOU'VE SUCCESSFULLY SECURED THE COMMITMENTS to Explore, Change, Collaborate, Build Consensus, and Invest from your prospective client. It's time for you to present your proposed solution to all stakeholders involved in decision making. You might be used to handing your prospect a proposal, presenting your solution, thanking him for his time, then disappearing until he gets back to you with his decision. After all, it's now up to the prospect to decide whether or not to buy, right?

Wrong. If you stop here, you are ceding control of the process. You are still a couple of commitments away from the decision. The sales process and your responsibilities don't end when you finish your presentation. If you don't want to go through the entire sales process only to hear, "I'm sorry. We've decided to go in a different direction," you'll need to ensure that you get a yes when you ask for the Commitment to Decide.

How do you do that? You secure the Commitment to Review—that is, to review your proposed solution *before* it takes its final form. Think of it as securing a preproposal meeting review. You'll present your preliminary solution to all stakeholders so they can review it and give feedback. The feedback will allow you to make changes to your solution and try again. Who ever said you have to get the answer right the first time? Once you know what your stakeholders are thinking, you can make adjustments so you can be sure you've tailored a solution that will be exactly right for your prospective client.

ANOTHER BITE OF THE APPLE

Who made the decision that you can only present your solution and your proposal one time? In a formal process, you will get only one chance to present. But otherwise there is nothing to stop you from asking for a review of your ideas as many times as it takes to get things right.

You may, of course, find some resistance. Some prospects will let each competitor present only once, in the interest of maintaining a "fair process." You might respond by saying:

I appreciate your commitment to a fair process. In our industry, it is customary for people to do the work to collaborate and build a unique program for their clients. If no one has asked you for this, it's because it isn't how they do this work. We would never suggest that you do anything unfair, but we do need these meetings to produce better results. Can we ask you for one review meeting before we provide our final proposal? We care deeply about getting things right, and later that may be what you appreciate most about us.

I know this might sound like a lot of words, but they may give you that second bite of the apple.

ELIMINATE THE ODDS OF HEARING NO

I once heard a story about the billionaire entrepreneur Ross Perot, who built a company called EDS. When Perot was nearing the decision stage with a prospective client, he liked to gather all the stakeholders in a boardroom and pass out his proposal, along with red pens and highlighters. He would tell them he'd done his very best to build the exact solution they needed, but he was afraid it wasn't exactly right. He wasn't sure that he hadn't missed anything, or that together they hadn't overlooked something important. He then asked the stakeholders to review the solution and highlight anything they thought needed changing to make it perfect. After the meeting, he would make the suggested modifications. And then he'd come back another day to present the revised solution.

Why did Perot go to all this trouble? Because he didn't want to get a no from his prospective clients. How did he ensure that his prospective clients would say yes? He showed up and asked them if it was exactly right. And when it wasn't, he made changes.

I don't know if this story is true or not, but it's one of the most powerful techniques I have ever used to win big opportunities—a combination of controlling the process, serving prospective clients by making sure they get what they need, collaborating, and building consensus. No wonder it works so well!

There is no value created for anyone if you come up with the wrong answer. You will simply have wasted everyone's time, including your own. So always test your solution to see if it will garner a yes before you ask for a final decision. To get the Commitment to Review, you might say to your prospect, "I want to make certain we get this exactly right and have a chance to dial this in for everyone on your team. When can we get everyone together to review our ideas and get their feedback, so we can make changes?"

Naturally, it's always difficult to get everyone together, especially more than once. Various stakeholders may be located in different time zones spread throughout the country or even around the world. Or your prospective client may have a practice of gathering the stakeholders and rotating all proposing companies through the boardroom in a day or two to present their solutions. Calling another meeting is out of the question. If you can't get everyone together, ask if you can do the preproposal meetings separately.

You might say, "I know it's really difficult for you to get everyone in a room together at one time. But I don't want to leave anyone out or deprive them of the opportunity to help us dial this in. I'll call or meet with people individually to get their feedback and modifications; then I'll review their changes with you. Will that work?"

Notice that you are telling your contacts that *you* will do the work and review it with them later. This way, they continue to collaborate and be active participants in deciding what comes next, even though they aren't on these calls. And if someone tells you, "I'd like to be part of those calls," be welcoming. Say, "Excellent! Let's pick some time slots when we can get people together on a video conference to get their feedback and ideas. What works?"

GIVE THEM SOMETHING THEY CAN SAY YES TO

During one of my preproposal meetings, a number of stakeholders asked me challenging questions about how my company would handle certain scenarios—situations that had gone wrong for them in the past. In a team sales situation like this one, I've found that it's a good idea to have a scribe, someone who writes down the questions that are asked and who asks them. Then you can go back and address them later in a more formal way.

After the meeting, I met with a number of the stakeholders to better understand their challenges and refine our approach to solving them. I sent two others from my team to meet with a few more members of the prospect's team to do the same. When we were done, all of us went back into the boardroom and shared our ideas. My team addressed each stakeholder question individually, making absolutely sure that the answer was right for them. It was abundantly clear that we cared about getting things right for them. And that made it easy for them to say yes, which they did. Since that time, that yes has generated about $20 million and that company is still one of our clients today. What lengths would you go to to produce $20 million in revenue? Does a second meeting to resolve concerns seem like too much?

Your goal should always be to craft a solution and a proposal to which your prospective client can only say yes. If it takes you two or three times through this cycle to dial in your solution and make it exactly right, then go through those cycles. It's better to have multiple meetings and win than a single meeting and lose.

At the end of each meeting, you might say, "Thank you so much for letting us present our solution. After having made a number of changes together, we think it's exactly right now. But if it isn't, we'll get together with you again to make changes."

GAINING THE COMMITMENT TO REVIEW

Your prospective client may resist the Commitment to Review for a multitude of reasons, and you may never really know why. But a response you might often get is something like, "Can you e-mail me your proposal and pricing?"

Many prospects try to get you to send your proposal and pricing by e-mail in lieu of having a meeting. But that requires you to completely give up control of the process and eliminates your ability to collaborate, get feedback, and make changes to your proposal. If something isn't quite right, you'll never know what it is, or that you need to do something different. You're not asking to present your final offer here. You're asking for the opportunity to get it right.

In response, you can say, "Of course I'll provide you with my proposal and investment details, but first I want to make sure it's completely dialed in and exactly the right solution. Can I show you and your team what we have at this point and get your feedback so I can make changes before we provide you with a final proposal?"

If you have to send an e-mail because your clients are too far away for you to see them in person, you still need to control the process and gain the Commitment to Review.

You might say, "I will absolutely send the proposal to you by e-mail. I am going to need to get your feedback in a couple of areas, and you may want to make a few modifications, even though I think we're really close. Let's schedule a twenty-minute call to review the proposal, and I'll send you the proposal before that call." Then send the proposal five minutes before the call.

Never give up control of the process. You know what happens when you cede control: Your dream client goes dark, avoiding your calls and e-mails. Once you give them what they believe they need to make a decision, they believe they won't need your input anymore. Nothing could be further from the truth.

Reviewing Is Crucial

Working together with the stakeholders to make sure your solution hits the bull's-eye is the only way you can be certain it will be something they'll agree to move forward with. Be aware, however, that most companies will expect you to present your solution, then go away while they decide what to do next. That's why you need to secure a commitment to review your proposal, which serves you, your company, *and* the prospective client and stakeholders, while allowing you to control the process.

COMMIT TO TAKE ACTION

Review these scripts and answer the questions that follow.

REVIEW I

Salesperson: Here is what our solution looks like now. The current state is that you have a throughput problem that is causing you to spend more to produce your product than budgeted, and the long cycle time is costing you orders and clients that are defecting for one of your competitor's products.

Salesperson: The future state we are working toward will have you doubling your throughput and meeting your client's needs.

Salesperson: To do that, we are going to invest something close to $775,000 to change the machine you are using now, and we are going to change one of your core processes. Here is what that's going to look like.

Salesperson: This is a timeline showing the milestones we'll pass through on the way to producing the results you need. What are we missing?

Operations stakeholder: We've never used a process like the one you are describing. We don't believe it will work as well as what we're doing now.

Salesperson: You are right to not believe it. The way you are set up now, it would never work. If I were you, I wouldn't agree to move forward with something like this without more evidence that it's going to work for you. And I might want to make some changes to make it fit my team's needs. What's the best way for you to look at this so we can make sure you are 100 percent comfortable moving forward?

Operations stakeholder: I want to see it in a production environment. I'd need a couple of my key people to see it too.

Salesperson: Would visiting one of my clients to see the solution and production environment and speaking with some of their people help you? Or is there something else that would work better?

Operations stakeholder: That would work. What challenges have you had propping up a solution like this?

Salesperson: We always struggle when we change this process. It takes a couple of weeks to dial in the solution, and it can be frustrating for people who haven't gone through the process. It's slower than we wish it were, but it's the only way we know how to get it right.

Operations stakeholder: It can't be worse than what we are doing now.

Salesperson: For two weeks or so, it can be worse. After it's dialed in, it's way better.

Prospective client: I am worried about your timeline. The milestones you are using have us making this transition during our peak season. We can't afford to miss deadlines during this time. We'll only be making matter worse. That's not going to work.

Salesperson: Does that mean we need to go before or after this period?

Operations stakeholder: If we had this solution before our peak, it would make peak a lot easier.

Prospective client: Is that possible?

Salesperson: Let me get with my team and recast the timelines to meet your dates. If we go before peak, I would worry about the changeover. It might mean you invest a little more to have our team on-site during the first few weeks to ensure we get you up and running. There are always unexpected challenges. Does it make sense to look at that?

Prospective client: I think so. Can you show us what you could do before and after our peak?

REVIEW II

Salesperson: You have now seen the solution in a production environment and we have new dates to review. This is what the solution looks like now, should we implement before your peak.

Prospective client: It makes sense to me, and it looks really good. We are going to want to get together and talk things over, and we'll get back to you.

Salesperson: That's perfect. As you go through this together, you are going to have questions and concerns, and I want to be here to serve you through that process. Can we schedule a meeting for next Wednesday, and I'll be available to address any concerns and answer any questions that come up during your conversations?

Prospective client: Sure, that makes sense. What time on Wednesday?

Questions:
1. At what stage do you normally cede control of the process to your prospective client?
2. What deals have you lost that might have been avoided had you gathered feedback and made adjustments to your proposal?
3. What do you need to do to incorporate a review meeting into your existing process?

Can I ask you to commit to studying the Commitment to Resolve Concerns right now?

Chapter 11

THE COMMITMENT TO RESOLVE CONCERNS

A FRIEND OF MINE WHO OWNS A SMALL SOFTWARE COMPANY asked me to join him and his partner on a sales call. Not being a salesperson, he was unsure how to handle it. So I agreed to lead the "sales" part of the call, while he and his partner demonstrated their software.

As I prepped my friend and his partner for the call, I gave them a preview of the language I was going to use to open the call. "I'll say something like: Thank you for meeting with us. Today, we are going to give you the software demo you requested, and we'll show you the total solution. At the end of this meeting, we'll schedule a follow-up meeting so we can address all of your concerns and make sure you are 100 percent confident with a decision to move forward."

My friend was horrified. "That is way too salesy," he said. "It's too aggressive. I don't want you to say anything that sounds like that." To a non-salesperson, the very softest of all language choices can sound aggressive, particularly if you are suggesting the process and asking for a commitment.

I asked him to share with me how he opens sales calls, and he admitted he didn't have any real experience selling. Then I asked him to trust me and promised him that his prospect wouldn't be offended. Reluctantly, he agreed.

When we met with the group of stakeholders, I opened the call exactly as I'd described. When I was finished, the main contact said, "That sounds great," and I handed the meeting over to my friend. Once the demo was completed, I addressed the group again, saying, "That's a lot to take in, and I am sure you're going to want to get together as a group to discuss it. We'd like to be here to answer any questions you have and address any concerns that come up as you go through this process. Can we meet again next week at this same time?" The main contact replied, "Yes, that would be very helpful," then turned to her team and asked, "Does that work for everybody?"

The following week, we came in for the meeting and the group shared a list of their questions and concerns. My friend addressed those concerns, and a week later was awarded their business.

What I did was to secure the Commitment to Resolve Concerns, which gave my friend a chance to answer the team's questions and assuage any fears that the deal might be anything other than great for all involved. This was absolutely crucial to the successful closing of the deal.

THE PROCESS DOESN'T END WHERE YOU THINK IT DOES

One huge but common mistake that sales professionals make is presenting the solution and failing to gain the next commitment. The prospective client says something like, "This looks great. We'll look it over and get back to you in a couple of weeks." The salesperson smiles, shakes hands with everyone, and leaves, not recognizing that that may be the end of the deal.

That's because the process of buying and selling doesn't end once you've made your presentation. Your prospective client needs you to help them assess their risks, address their concerns, and eliminate their fears. That's the reason so many of them don't buy immediately after you present. They don't need time to look over your proposal; time has never helped anyone make a better decision. They need more information and better counsel.

I've found that the nature and number of a prospect's fears and concerns are directly proportional to the risk and the size of the investment. The greater the risk or investment, the more concerns and the deeper they will be. This is completely natural. Aren't you especially concerned and in need of greater assurances when you make a major purchase, like buying a house or car? Don't you want to be sure, before you commit to making a big investment, that it's going to work for you, that you haven't overlooked something, and that you aren't going to be surprised, embarrassed, or dismayed down the line? Of course you do. Your prospects feel the same way.

"Then why," you might ask, "don't they bring up these fears and concerns after my presentation?" There may be several reasons: They didn't want to embarrass themselves or you. They didn't want you to try to "sell them," to pressure them to act in spite of their fears and doubts (one of the reasons the word "sales" developed a negative connotation). Or they were simply uncomfortable talking about these issues. If you leave the meeting without gaining the Commitment to Resolve Concerns, the fears, doubts, and concerns remain unaddressed, and your prospect may decide not to move forward with your solution.

FEARS AND CONCERNS, REAL AND IMAGINED

One of the primary tasks of the human mind is to assess risks and direct the body to take action with the goal of keeping you alive. And it's exceptionally good at identifying these risks, even when they don't really exist. So when you leave your prospective clients alone to make decisions, they can ask themselves all kinds of questions about what might go wrong and how it could harm them. Here are a few of the most common ones and the underlying fears:

Is this too much money to spend?

Your prospect knows that if he makes this deal he will be spending more money, yet he's not convinced he'll get the outcomes he needs. He's afraid of wasting company money. This may be especially true if he's made bad deals in the past, in which the supplier didn't deliver the promised results.

Am I being taken advantage of?

Nobody wants to be a patsy. Your prospective client doesn't know what you're charging your other clients for these outcomes. If he accepts your proposal, is he being played for a fool? He needs to do right by his company, especially when it comes to investing money.

Is this really going to work?

Every time your prospect agrees to a deal, it is because the salesperson has made him believe that the product, service, or solution is going to work. But that doesn't always turn out to be true. And even when he is partially responsible for the failure, the prospect will fear that most, or all, salespeople and their companies will fail him.

Am I going to be embarrassed by having made this decision?

If your prospective client makes a deal with you and fails to produce the desired outcomes, he will feel humiliated in front of his superiors, peers, and employees. This is especially true when highly visible change initiatives are involved, and the price of failing to achieve the promised results can lead to the loss of one's job.

Will the people who are affected by this decision revolt if something goes wrong?

Your prospective client may worry that there will be too many problems and complaints from those who have to implement a significant change.

Can I trust that the salesperson will be here for me when something goes wrong?

Your prospective client may wonder what you will do to help him if "the train comes off the tracks." Salespeople in the past who promised to deliver may have run for the hills at the first sign of real trouble. He doesn't want to be left with a mess on his hands and no one to help him.

Can I push the decision off for a couple of months and see what happens?

Making a commitment now means changing now. If your prospect believes he needs to change but is afraid of all the ramifications, pushing the decision off allows him the luxury of not saying yes but not killing the deal either. He doesn't have to pay any consequences, at least for the time being.

Would it be easier to keep doing what we're doing instead of dealing with all of this?

Change can be complicated, political, and messy. Change takes time and energy, both of which are typically in short supply. Your prospective client may be wondering, "Is this worth it?"

It doesn't matter whether or not these fears and concerns are based on truth. To your dream clients they are very real. You must convince them that their investment will be worth the results and that your price matches the value you are creating. You must assure them that what you sell is going to work and that you will be there to ensure that they achieve the desired outcomes. And not only are they *not* going to be embarrassed, they will look like winners for having made such an innovative and effective change. And you must assure them that they *do* really need to change now.

PROVIDING PROOF THAT YOU'LL BE AN EXCELLENT PARTNER

One of the less obvious but very important benefits to gaining the Commitment to Resolve Concerns—and then resolving those concerns—is that your prospect will be able to observe firsthand the kind of partner you'll be. He'll see for himself that you will be there to help him with difficult decisions, answer his questions, offer advice, and solve problems. While other salespeople disappear after making their presentations, you stay engaged, involved, and available. This will help to create a preference for you, your company, and your solution in your prospect's mind.

You might believe that you've already provided the proof that would dispatch any fears or doubts your dream client might have conjured up during this process. Call me skeptical. It's more likely that you have been taught to present proof too soon or in a way that doesn't address your client's real concerns.

Too Soon

One of the worst things you can do is provide proof too soon. In fact, some salespeople still open their first sales call by presenting who their company is, what they do, and how they are different from their competitors. They want to provide proof as to why their dream client should choose them over their competitors. They want to prove that they are worth talking to, regardless of the fact that their dream client is not going to determine how valuable the meeting was based on anything other than the value the salesperson traded for it. Your company history isn't value.

The problem with providing proof that you are worth doing business with too soon is that it assumes that your dream client is trying to decide whether or not to buy from you. They aren't concerned about whether or not you are the right partner yet, because they have made no commitment to change and, as you know, that commitment comes first.

In the early stages of the sales process, who you are and how you help your dream client is greater proof that you belong there than anything you can tell your client about your company and the logos you've won.

Providing proof later in the process, during the presentation, can still be too soon. If you open your presentation with a picture of your building and an organizational chart, you are trying to provide proof that your dream client should choose your company before you present what is most important to them: their challenge and how you intend to help them with it.

If you show your prospective client a slide full of the logos of the major brands you serve during your proposal and presentation, you are providing proof that they should choose you because other companies have. There are better ways to do this, like using some of your clients as case studies to demonstrate how you helped them with challenges and what you learned as you worked together.

The reason your prospective client doesn't care about how long your company has been in business, who sits on your board, and whom you work with is because they aren't looking for this proof. Look, I am not suggesting that you aren't going to need this proof in your slide deck. What I am saying is that if you think you are addressing your dream client's fears and doubts this way, you are mistaken. If you are still in the game and presenting, they already believe you belong there. Their concerns, however, lie somewhere else.

When you present your proof too soon, it isn't tied to the concerns your dream client has about moving forward with you, your solution, or the change they are considering.

Proof of What?

The way to provide proof is to connect it to your dream client's concerns. When you provide proof, you need to answer the question being asked of you. It doesn't do you any good to provide proof that addresses the wrong concerns.

Your dream client may be concerned about making the decision to move forward because they still aren't sure that they should change now. A picture of the logos of the companies that you work with and a letter of recommendation from a major client don't address this concern, do they? This concern needs to be resolved in a meeting where you and your dream client review the case for change and explore what they risk by not changing now.

In larger, complex deals that come with some risk, money is always going to be a concern. Is it too much money? Is it right to spend this money now, or should it be invested somewhere else in the business? Even when you have no competitor, in big deals you are still competing with different initiatives, many of which require a financial investment. You have to address the concern over whether this is the right initiative at all.

If your prospective client is concerned about your ability to execute, you have to provide proof that gives them 100 percent confidence that you will deliver the outcomes you are selling them.

ASKING FOR THE COMMITMENT TO RESOLVE CONCERNS

If you don't leave your presentation meeting with a signed contract, assume that your deal is at risk, and ask your prospective client for the Commitment to Resolve Concerns. By now you know that if there are concerns, you'll need to be there to resolve them.

You say, "As you discuss this with your team, you are no doubt going to have questions and concerns. I want to make sure that I am here to address those questions and concerns for you. How do you look at this same time next week?"

Setting up a follow-up meeting is a win-win situation for you. If the team has questions or concerns, you can resolve them and ask again to move forward. If there are no real questions or concerns, you are going to have a very productive meeting talking about next steps.

But let's say your prospect replies, "We'll get back to you after we meet, should we need anything."

You know that the buyer's process doesn't end at that point. And you know that your prospective client's team will have concerns and questions.

So you say, "Can I share one idea with you and make a recommendation?"

Pause here and wait until your prospect agrees, then continue.

"A lot of the questions and concerns that come up when our clients meet with their teams are technical or have to do with how we will respond to their needs or challenges. If we are there to answer these questions, they will get a better understanding of our commitment to them. I recognize you want time with your team, but can I ask you for the opportunity to come in to address any questions or concerns at the end of that meeting?"

If all goes well, your prospective client will agree to the Commitment to Resolve Concerns and you'll be one major step closer to closing the deal. If not, persist and ask again for a follow-up meeting. I can't overstate how important this is.

WHAT HAPPENS WHEN YOU AREN'T THERE TO RESOLVE CONCERNS?

If you aren't there to help your prospective client address his fears and resolve his concerns, someone else will be. Your client will likely look first to someone on his team. That person may give him good counsel, or reinforce his fears. Or the client may look to someone who isn't engaged in the process and who has no idea what's at stake or how important it is for your prospect to change *now*. That person may actually create new concerns. Whoever steps in to fill this role has the capability of damaging or destroying the work you and your prospective client have done together.

You may also leave the door open for a competitor. I once lost a $2 million account after gaining a verbal commitment from a prospective client. Unbeknownst to me, a competitor had engaged him toward the end of my sales process and showed him something I hadn't. I was stunned when the prospect told me he had awarded his business to my competitor, and I insisted on a meeting.

During this meeting, the client explained the part of my competitor's program that had appealed to him most. I showed him five pages of meeting notes as proof that the challenge this program addressed never came up in any of our meetings. He said, "I know. But when I saw it, I liked it."

Six months later I won the prospect back from my competitor, who had failed to deliver the results he had promised. The upshot was that the client had spent six months and one million dollars without getting what he really wanted, while my company went six months without the million dollars that would have gone to us had I assumed there was still a competitive threat asking for the last bite at the apple.

So do whatever you can to set a meeting to resolve questions and concerns. Your prospect may respond to your request with something like, "We have two more proposals to look at before we decide. We'll get back to you with a decision." In that case, you reply, "Thank you so much. I feel very strongly that we are the right partner for you here, and I believe that no one else is going to produce the same results we will. As you look at other proposals, you may see different ideas that you like that may or may not work for you. Can we schedule a meeting to answer any questions and address anything else you need to know before you move forward?"

Gaining the Commitment to Resolve Concerns is every bit as important as any of the other nine commitments, and it may be the one that causes more losses to competitors and to the status quo.

ONE STEP CLOSER

Resolving your prospective client's concerns by satisfactorily answering their questions, affirming their need to make a change *now*, and explaining how your solution will deliver his desired outcomes in the most efficient, proficient way possible is a major part of the sales process. Don't just make your presentation and cross your fingers. Get that extra meeting and show that your solution is the only way to go!

COMMIT TO TAKE ACTION

Review this script and answer the questions that follow.

Prospective client: We had a couple of questions come up. First, we understand the need to invest more here, but we want to know if we have any options to pay for the equipment over a longer period than you showed us.

Salesperson: There are other options. Can you share with me why this is important to you now?

Prospective client: We don't have the entire budget for the capital expenses in this year.

Salesperson: What would you need to make it work for you?

Prospective client: We'd need to move $150,000 into next year.

Salesperson: Okay. Let me see what we can do for you there.

Operations stakeholder: We are worried about the training. How much time does it take for someone to get up to speed using your process? If we miss by a little when it comes to timing, we could fall behind.

Salesperson: It takes a couple of weeks. I am not sure how to resolve your concern, but I can share some ideas with you. We could have some of our people here to help. Or we could have some of your key people trained prior to going live. What would make you confident here?

Operations stakeholder: Nothing. I get paid to worry.

Salesperson: I understand. What do you want to do?

Operations stakeholder: Both. Can we have my key people trained before we switch things over and have your people here during the first couple of weeks?

Salesperson: That makes sense. We'll make changes to reflect that in the solution. Anything else?

Prospective client: No. Other than these two issues, it's perfect.

Salesperson: Can I make these changes and bring back the proposal, a contract, and a documented plan of how we'll move forward together?

Questions:

1. In most of your deals, who controls the process after you present your solution?
2. Think back over deals you've lost. What concerns were left unaddressed that might have been easily resolved had you gained the Commitment to Resolve Concerns?
3. What proof can you provide that would eliminate those concerns? When—and how—should you be prepared to resolve those concerns?

If there is nothing else for us to cover, I'd like to ask you for the commitment to read the next chapter with me.

Chapter 12

THE COMMITMENT TO DECIDE

THE COMMITMENT TO DECIDE IS SIMPLY AN AGREEMENT BE-
tween you and the prospective client that the two of you will act together to achieve specific outcomes. It changes your relationship, transforming your prospect into a client and you into a partner.

There was a time when securing this agreement—otherwise known as "closing the deal"—was believed to be the most important and challenging part of selling. Every salesperson worth his salt had a copy of Zig Ziglar's *Secrets of Closing the Sale* and Tom Hopkins's *How to Master the Art of Selling*, both of which subscribed to this idea. But today we live in different times that call for a different approach.

The Commitment to Decide (once thought of as the *only* "close") might actually be one of the easier commitments you obtain, provided you have gained the prior commitments. But if you've skipped any of them, it's going to be challenging because it will be difficult for your dream client to say yes when there is still so much work left undone. So the Commitment to Decide will be either your easiest or your most difficult commitment to get, depending on the groundwork you've laid.

THE EASIEST OR MOST DIFFICULT COMMITMENT

If you haven't done everything necessary to have earned the right to ask your client to give you their business, you have made closing unnecessarily difficult.

- Maybe you are uncomfortable asking your prospective clients to make the Commitment to Change. Maybe you believe because you have a contact or two engaged with you that the decision to change has already been made. Countless so-called opportunities are never closed because the salesperson didn't gain this commitment.
- Perhaps you don't really want to collaborate on a solution, choosing instead to show your prospect your very best idea, strongly believing you know exactly how to get them the results they need. Maybe you don't want their input. Every day, prospects refuse offers because they don't match their needs.
- Maybe you're scared to death to build consensus, having brought other stakeholders into a conversation in the past, only to have them blow up your deal with their infighting and internal disagreements. More deals are being lost to the status quo because of a lack of consensus.
- Discussing the investment before we get to contracts? Forget about it! Why bring up that topic before you absolutely must? So you say, but if you don't want to lose to a lower-priced competitor or discount, buck up and talk about the investment.

Here's the thing: If you don't gain all the commitments you need leading up to this point, you are increasing the likelihood of hearing no. You haven't done what was necessary to have earned an easy yes.

You can have a few discovery meetings, provide a proposal, and then hear nothing for weeks or months because your dream client hasn't committed to change. Your pipeline may have a number of "opportunities" that fall into this category, and now you know why. You might have the perfect solution, but if your prospective client believes there is a better solution—one that takes into account the things they want—you are going to hear no when you ask for the business. Deservedly so.

You may not want to offend the contact you are working with by insisting that you bring the rest of their team into the conversation, but when your proposal is put in front of the stakeholders you've neglected and it's the first time they've seen it, you can expect that they will forcefully reject it. This is true even when what you sell will benefit them! By neglecting these stakeholders, you have proved you don't care about them.

Your solution is going to cost what it costs no matter when you disclose the amount. Your price doesn't drop the longer you hide it. It just creates greater sticker shock. I know what you are thinking: "I want to build the value of the solution so they believe it's worth the investment." The problem with that approach is that if you are more expensive than your competitors, you aren't being compared against the greater value you create. You are being compared against competitive offerings and alternatives. It's easier to sell your higher price by justifying the investment earlier. You'll also find you won't have to discount your solution nearly as often or as much when you build the value throughout the process.

You make it easy to ask for the commitment to buy from you when you gain all the necessary commitments before you ask for the Commitment to Decide. By asking for—and obtaining—the more difficult commitments you need throughout the sales process, you make asking for this final decision one of the easiest decisions to obtain. By avoiding these commitments, you make it more difficult.

HOW TO ASK FOR THE COMMITMENT TO DECIDE

I don't have to tell you how important it is to get a yes to this commitment, or how good it feels to win a new client. This is a big deal. That being said, there's no reason to think that this ask requires special techniques or tactics. Just be yourself and treat your prospective client the same way you've treated her throughout the sales process.

Use Natural Language

Memorizing special closing techniques or using tactical approaches will just sound false to your prospect and erode her trust. So ask for her business in your own natural language and be as direct as possible.

You might say, "I believe we've done everything we've needed to do up to this point, and unless you believe we need to do something else, I'd like to ask you for your business. Can we get started?"

There is nothing tactical, tricky, or manipulative about this approach. Here's another way to put it: "Can we begin putting this solution in place for you now?" Or you can say: "I think we've addressed all of your concerns and have a good plan in place. All we need to get started is your approval and a signed agreement. Does this work for you?"

What Not to Say

Whatever you do, be sure to avoid using any coy, convoluted, or tricky approaches when asking for your prospect's business. Here are a few examples of what *not* to say:

If I could provide you with this solution at this price, is there anything that would prevent you from doing business with me?

This isn't a close; it's not even a request for a commitment. It's the kind of language a salesperson uses when he's afraid of asking for a commitment. He's asking to resolve concerns while simultaneously suggesting that another price is available, which opens up the possibility of negotiation and can make the prospect worry that the investment may be too high.

Is my company the kind of company you want to work with? Am I the kind of salesperson you want to work with? If money wasn't an issue, would you buy this right now?

Tie-downs like these are self-oriented and intentionally manipulative. A bad salesperson asked me these questions once, and I said yes to the first and no to the second, noting that money wasn't an issue. Obviously, this wasn't the outcome he expected. But he made the choice to use this poor closing language, so I made the choice to reject that language with extreme prejudice.

When should we get started?

This is another way to avoid asking directly for a prospect's business. The hope is that the prospect will respond, "Right away." But more likely the answer will be, "Let me think about it."

If you buy today, I can discount our proposal by X amount and give you [an extra service] at no additional cost. Does that sound good to you?

This might work in an infomercial. But it's an abysmal approach for a professional salesperson. (I actually cringed when I typed that approach.) If a prospect agrees to buy, it should be because of the good work you've done, not because you are offering a discount or giving away freebies.

If you've gained all the commitments you need, it's almost certain that you can expect yes, and that you earned it! Your confidence in asking your prospective client for his business can be directly proportional to your confidence in the work you've done up to this point.

WHAT IF THEY SAY NO?

Of course, it's always possible that your dream client will say no to going forward with your solution. It happens. That's because selling is more akin to mixed martial arts than it is to boxing. In boxing, world champions may go undefeated for decades. But in mixed martial arts you can be a world champion having won five fights and lost five fights. Losses are expected, even if you hate losing.

If your prospective client says no, it's quite likely that she'll follow it with a reason. Not a problem. If she needs to do or have something else before moving forward, help her do or get it, if at all possible.

If she doesn't give you a reason, be prepared to say, "If you aren't ready to move forward, that means we haven't done something we still need to do or something has changed on your end. Can you share with me what you're thinking?"

Don't get defensive, act surprised, or let on that you're unhappy that you didn't get what you wanted. Something went wrong. You need to find out what that is and try to do whatever you can to make it right.

COMMON CONCERNS

If you've gained all the commitments you need up to this point, you aren't likely to get many objections. Your prospective client has agreed to change, so they shouldn't suddenly suggest that they aren't moving forward. You've collaborated and built a consensus, so there shouldn't be any concerns about making this change or what it involves. You discussed the investment early on, so no one should have sticker shock over the price. And since you resolved all of your prospect's concerns, it's unlikely that they are going to spring anything new on you.

And yet there may still be some concerns that keep the deal from going through. Here are two of the most common ones:

We're not sure we are ready to move forward.

Sometimes people get cold feet coming down the home stretch. Your prospect may worry about what could go wrong and try to stall a decision. You can say, "All of the issues that brought us to this point are still here, and they are still relevant. I am afraid that by not moving forward, things will get worse. What's the best way for us to resolve this issue together?"

Or you might say, "Can you share with me what's changed for you?" If something has changed, you won't be able to help your prospective client until you know what it is. Only then can you say, "How do you think we should deal with this so that we can move forward together?"

Your prospect's concerns won't go away if you ignore them. They will only grow bigger and more menacing. In order to move forward, you need to get the prospect to put them on the table so you can dispatch them.

We love everything about this, but we're going to need you to lower your price.

You say, "I understand that you have a responsibility to your company to get the most value for your money, and that is what we've done here. By taking money out of this program, we open ourselves up to risk, and we put some of the outcomes we've discussed in jeopardy. This is the right investment for this solution, but if we missed something here, I am happy to go back and rework the solution to come up with a different investment. Does it make sense to move forward with this plan, or should we come up with something else?"

Do *not* say, "We are in business to make a profit" or "Let me go back and ask my sales manager if we can do better." Remember, those who buy for a company are only doing their job when they ask you to sharpen your pencil, and they have to be sure you are being honest about your price. Since so many sales organizations raise their prices by the amount they expect to discount, your prospect has been trained to ask.

MORE THAN ONE COMMITMENT

Let's say you've won the day and gotten a solid yes from your prospective client—who is now your client and partner. Congratulations! Just be aware that the Commitment to Decide comes with a lot of smaller commitments, which you'll still need to obtain. Here are some typical ones:

Exchanging and reviewing contracts

At some point, either you will provide your new client with your contract or they will provide you with theirs. Do your utmost to gain another Commitment for Time to get together to review and discuss any changes. If you don't schedule an appointment, you are likely to find yourself waiting weeks or even months to acquire the signatures.

You can say, "We can have these documents reviewed by Wednesday next week. Can we schedule a half hour next Thursday afternoon to walk through any areas we need to discuss?"

Control the process and you can influence the outcome.

Moving contracts through legal

Legal departments are typically swamped with litigation over complex legal matters and may put off attending to your contract. Try to gain control of this process by saying, "Can we schedule a quick call with your legal department before we provide them with contracts to review? In my experience, if they don't see the dates we have agreed to, they may put this on the back burner. If we can get them on the phone, we can make sure they know our timeline."

Implementation meetings

Bringing your team to implementation meetings allows you to begin the handoff from you to your team, and from your contacts to their team, to assure a smooth transition.

You might say, "One of the ways we make sure we get started right is with a series of kickoff meetings that allow us to work through the implementation and speed up the results. I'd like to start scheduling those meetings so we can hit the ground running. Can we set the first one for next week?"

Committing to a start date

Most salespeople would not dream of asking a prospect what date she would want to begin implementing the solution until they have the Commitment to Decide. But I think it should happen much earlier, around the time the Commitment to Change is secured. I believe it's best to ask for the commitment to a start date as early in the process as possible, as long as you have earned it. But no matter when you decide to ask for it, you might broach the subject by simply asking, "What date would you like us to start the implementation?"

You've hit a home run by securing the Commitment to Decide, but don't neglect to gain these additional commitments as well. They'll ensure that your partnerships gets off to a smooth start and you'll be ready to execute in a timely manner.

COMMIT TO TAKE ACTION

Review this script and answer the questions that follow.

Salesperson: This is the final solution and investment. I think we are in good shape to move forward, unless there is still something you need. If there isn't anything you need, can we go ahead and get started?

Prospective client: We have what we need. What do we need to do to get started?

That's it. There are no fancy closing techniques here. Nor are there a hundred ways to ask for the sale that would cause you to lose credibility with your dream client or violate their trust. There is no assumption that asking for the business will be difficult because, having

---

done the necessary work of gaining the commitments you need throughout the entire process, it is almost always the easiest commitment to gain.

Questions:
1. What commitments do you normally skip that make asking for the final commitment more difficult for you?
2. How does skipping these commitments make it more difficult for your client to say yes later in the process?
3. You may never have been asked to do this before, but it's important. Write down the words you will use to ask for the Commitment to Decide. What do you normally say?

For you to reap the rewards of what you have done up to this point, you are going to begin using the work here in your daily life. Will you try something from this book tomorrow?

Chapter 13

THE COMMITMENT
TO EXECUTE

YOU SOLD YOUR DREAM CLIENT A PRODUCT, SERVICE, OR SOLU-
tion and promised certain outcomes, which means you are the one
responsible for ensuring that those outcomes are produced. This is referred to as execution, and it's crucial. If you want lifelong relationships,
repeat business, and the unshakable preference that prevents your clients
from even speaking to one of your competitors (yes, it happens!), you
must make sure that the outcomes you've sold them are executed.

A couple of major sticking points can arise during execution. First,
when there are serious challenges to producing the promised results,
your company may need to get involved. That is, you may need to get
the internal commitments necessary to produce those results. Second,
your client may need to implement certain changes necessary for producing those results. And even though they committed to this when
they made the decision to move forward, when the work begins, problems can follow.

Let's take a look at these two stumbling blocks and how you can
surmount them.

GAINING INTERNAL COMMITMENTS

Like it or not, if you're going to succeed in sales, you'll have to sell inside your own company as well as to your dream clients. You may hate internal politics, but you'll need to gain the commitments that allow you to execute, even when they come from people within your company. It's very much like gaining the commitments that lead to making a deal; you're just dealing with different prospects.

First you'll need to persuade the people who can help you to give you their time. Most likely they won't be working in sales; they'll belong to operations, management, and maybe even leadership. Then you'll need to give them a compelling reason to change, and a vision of the future. You'll have to explore change and collaborate with your team to develop ideas about making things work from your side.

You may say to your team, "I'm going to need your help with some issues we are having with this client. If we don't change what we are doing, we are putting their results, our relationship, and this deal at risk. I have some ideas about the changes we need to make and what we need to get done, but I'd like to hear from you first. What do we have to do to get this back on course, and what are you struggling with?"

You're going to have to be as other-oriented when working inside your company as you are when working outside. It's very difficult to deal with a failure on your side, and emotions run high when you sell something and your team doesn't deliver it. But you'll have to apply your sales skills to those inside your own company and help them get what they need to make things better. You can't attack them and then expect them to move heaven and earth for you.

Say something like, "Can I share something with you and ask you for a little bit of help?"

This is a hard request to refuse. Don't get angry or emotional. Don't complain. You are solving a problem. One of the most important rules of solving problems in business or in life is to focus on the problem, not the person.

Then explain: "We are struggling to produce results for a new client. I've met with our teams, and they need to change one internal process specifically for this client. They also need the budget to make this change. If we don't make this change, we can't produce the results we sold, and we'll likely end up in trouble with this client. Can you help me make the changes we need to make and help me find the money?"

And why wouldn't your own management team want to help you execute? Let me answer this for you: because they are as resistant to change as some of your clients; because you are suggesting that they spend money; or because it's easier to believe either you sold something your company couldn't deliver or it's the client's fault.

You can continue, "I've done a pretty good job of working with our teams to figure out what they need. I am sure they're telling me the truth. I have a responsibility to them, so I said I'd take the lead on this. I'll follow your lead if you want me to. What do you think we should do here?"

You have to be resourceful and use all your sales skills to make change happen in your own company. It may not be easy, but there is always a way.

And wait—there's more! You get to do this on the client's side too.

GAINING COMMITMENTS ON THE CLIENT'S SIDE

This is where things get fun. You're trying to produce the results you promised your client, but they aren't making the necessary changes, which is preventing you from producing. Maybe your client's team isn't doing what they need to do because they don't really want to. Maybe they're being obstinate because they don't want to change. Maybe the change is more difficult than they imagined, and they've gone back to doing things the old way. In truth, it doesn't matter why they aren't doing what they need to do. It's up to you to help them make the changes they need to make.

You'll find that some clients are more mature about commercial relationships than others. And the more mature they are, the easier it will be for you to overcome the challenges involved in producing the desired outcome. There have been times when I've had to inform a client that my company made a mistake that hurt them, only to be told by the client that they shared responsibility. I had another client who was so partner-oriented that even when I explained a particular error was 100 percent my fault, he wanted to know how his team could help prevent the problem from happening again. I only wish that every client were this partner-oriented.

But I have also had clients who were less mature and anything but partner-oriented, people who refused to make changes on their side because they believed that any problem was "always the vendor's fault." You may find that some clients will buy your equipment with every intention of using it, and then do nothing with it. Some will subscribe to your solution and place very few orders. One company I worked with sold a piece of equipment that produced better results than anything on the market. It allowed them to generate better results and greater profits. But some of their clients who bought it didn't want to ask their customers to pay for the better results the equipment produced. So the equipment sat and gathered dust.

Change is difficult. Change often means that you'll have to have difficult conversations and ask people to behave differently than they have in the past. And that takes time and a lot of emotional energy.

ASKING FOR THE COMMITMENT TO EXECUTE

Whether you're dealing with a dream client or one that is more of a problem, you'll have to obtain the Commitment to Execute in order to deliver the promised outcome. The starting point for obtaining this commitment is a meeting, hopefully with someone who understands the challenge and has enough clout to get something done. As always, be scrupulously professional; there should be no accusations, no blame, and no complaining.

You might say something like, "We are struggling to deliver the results we are working toward. I've made some changes on our end, but I am afraid we're going to continue to struggle unless we make a few changes on your side too. Can I share our view of what's happening and get your feedback?"

Language matters. You want to be soft and protect people's egos. If you make accusations, you can expect people to become defensive and respond poorly. You may want to take responsibility for what your client hasn't changed, by saying, "Even though we talked about the changes your team would have to make and agreed that they were necessary, I think we underestimated how difficult it was going to be. Can we talk about what we need to do to help your team and see if there is anything I can do on our side to make it easier for them?"

There is a lot in this statement. You have reminded your client that you talked about these changes. You admitted to underestimating how difficult it was going to be for them, and by doing so made sure that no one feels attacked or defensive. You assumed they still need to change, and you asked to see what you can do to make it easier. You focused on the problem, not the people.

You might say, "I know that the change we are asking you to make isn't easy for you. But we can't get the results we need if we don't make these changes. I want to make sure we do everything we can to help you. What can we do to help?"

If you found that gaining any of the ten commitments was troublesome, you haven't seen anything yet. One of my clients, a manufacturer, wanted to improve the caliber of their workforce. We recruited a very different-caliber employee than they were used to. We were recruiting differently, verifying backgrounds, and doing more than anyone else to prepare them for their new jobs. We were delivering the outcome we promised, until our employees stopped following the client's personal protective equipment rules. They were coming into the plant without their steel-toed shoes, choosing to wear tennis shoes so they could be comfortable. We didn't understand why this happened, so we made changes internally. We required every employee to bring their equipment in before starting the job, and we had our team monitoring compliance. The issues persisted, and we discovered that something else was wrong.

Our employees were working side by side with our client's employees. Their employees had long tenures, and they knew what they could and couldn't get away with at work. As they worked with our employees, they started to teach them the ropes. Our employees were violating the safety rules because they were watching and learning from our client's employees, who were also doing whatever they could not to have to wear their steel-toed shoes.

It wasn't enough for us to change on our end. We also had to ask our client to make changes on theirs. Asking your client to make the change necessary to execute is where things get sticky. At first, their management team was outraged that we would suggest that their people were to blame for our people not wearing their steel-toed shoes. It was a new relationship, and they didn't know us well enough to trust us as much as they later would. In one meeting, one of their managers shouted, "I demand to see your records. I want names and times when you saw our people not wearing their personal protective gear!" His vice president eventually told him to settle down, that everyone knew they had employees who colored outside the lines.

When we provided our meticulous records and proof, they softened. Then a number of their managers got together and discussed the fact that some of their people were skirting the rules. We both made additional changes, and we eventually ended up getting both our teams into compliance, which was the outcome we both needed. That's why you need the Commitment to Execute.

A WORD ON THE WORDS

I like soft language choices. You can be a "challenger" without being "challenging." Try never to use language that causes another person to believe he has to defend himself or his decisions. You should try to influence people to do what is in their best interests, knowing that if you put them on the defensive, you are working against that outcome.

Use language that builds trust. You should never want to do or say anything that is going to make someone want to withdraw from your relationship. That's why you should prefer to use language that is natural, straightforward, and professional. I don't like tips, tricks, or tie-downs. If what you say makes your client believe you are doing something *to* him, it isn't serving either of you.

The ideas and the language here might be uncomfortable to you at first. If you've never asked for some of these commitments, it will take a little time for them to become part of your repertoire. Just consider the things that I suggest you say as outlines, broad strokes that reflect the principles in this book. Then modify them to fit your personality and the kind of language that comes naturally to you.

AN AGENT FOR CHANGE

You are an agent for change. Because you sell, you must be a catalyst for transformation, modification, and modernization. To do this, you must also be a leader who ensures that the change you sell is successfully implemented. You must execute that change. And you can measure your own success by the outcomes you generate for your clients.

COMMIT TO TAKE ACTION

Review this script and answer the questions that follow.

Salesperson: We are struggling to produce the results we need here, and I have some ideas about why that is and what we might do. Can I share that with you?

Client: I agree! Our people aren't able to use what you've sold us. It isn't working. This is becoming a mess for us.

Salesperson: I've done some work to see where we've gone wrong here. Can I share what I have learned so far and ask you to fill in what I am missing?

Client (cautiously): Go ahead.

Salesperson: We knew training was going to be important, and we knew we would need our people on-site for some time. We weren't able to train some of your key people. A few of them weren't here when we did the training, and a few more were here, had the training, but aren't following the procedures they would need to follow for this to work. In my mind, there are two problems. One, we need to train the rest of your team, and then we need some help getting a few of your old guard to agree to change the process.

Client: You should have trained the people who weren't here.

Salesperson: I agree. I've already made arrangements for another training. I just need your permission to schedule it.

Client: We need to do this as soon as possible.

Salesperson: I'll take care of that. I am also concerned about getting the couple of people who aren't using the new process to change. What do we do there?

Client: I know who you are talking about. They've been here a long time. They're good employees, and they're set in their ways. Why can't they do it their way?

Salesperson: They are doing it their way. That's what actually causes the process to break down. This change is what is going to allow you to produce the results we're working toward.

Client: They're going to be a problem here. Isn't there some way they can continue to do this the way they've done it?

Salesperson: Not if we want the better results. Can I make a suggestion?

Client: Go ahead.

Salesperson: Can we meet with them as a group to share why this process has to change, give them some additional training, and create a certification process that allows them to be the certified trainers of the new process? If we can get their buy-in, explain how important it is to the company, and give them ownership, they retain their status on the floor and they can influence and direct others.

Client: I like that. I think it would work. What do you need from me?

Salesperson: I need you to have the person they respect the most ask them to agree to what we've decided here. I'll schedule the meetings and the trainings.

This is real life when you sell outcomes and when you are accountable for what you sell. Problems don't age well, and the longer they go unresolved, the more difficult it can be to turn things around. Your deal doesn't end when your client signs the contract. That's where it begins.

Questions:

1. What do you do when your new client struggles to produce results because they aren't making the changes they need to make?

2. What commitments do you need to ask for to help them execute and realize the results you sold them?

Chapter 14

GUIDELINES FOR CLOSING

THERE ARE NO RULES IN SELLING, AND YOU HAVE TO KNOW them all. What this means is that selling requires that you be thoughtful, you explore the choices available to you, and you make good decisions about the course of action upon which you decide. What works in one situation may or may not be met with success in future scenarios, even when they appear to be similar.

What follows in this chapter are not hard and fast rules. They are guidelines, ideas to be considered as you learn to gain commitments, adjust your approach, and master this critical skill set. Study these guidelines and use them to improve your ability to ask for—and gain—the commitments that you need.

UNDERSTAND ALL THE COMMITMENTS AND KNOW WHAT COMMITMENT YOU NEED

In most sales books, you will find hundreds of "closes" for the commitment to buy or to sign a contract, as if that were the only commitment necessary to win a deal. In small, simple, low-price, low-risk deals, that close may be all that is necessary. In larger, complex, expensive, strategic, and high-risk deals, a single close, regardless of how many ways you can ask, will not suffice.

This book is different. You now know the ten different commitments you need to gain as you help the buyer through their buying process and your sales process. In some of the chapters, there are multiple commitments that are rolled up to fit under a single chapter title because there may be more than one commitment necessary.

You can't move the final ask forward by skipping the asks that should have come before it. Deals stall when you don't ask for—or obtain—the commitment you need at each stage. Asking for commitments that you haven't earned or getting too far out in front of what your dream client is ready to commit to will actually slow your sales process, and it will prevent the client from benefiting from your solution sooner. You have to earn the right to ask for every commitment.

It is important for you to know what commitment you need to create or move an opportunity forward. What commitment best serves your client in moving forward and making change?

USE NATURAL LANGUAGE

If the language you use to close makes you feel bad about yourself, then it isn't good closing language. If your close has a name, then it probably isn't good for business-to-business sales.

I am not saying that asking for commitments won't sometimes make your prospective client uncomfortable. This book is built on the idea that we have to help our clients face the dangers—which are almost always greater than their fears. Your clients, however, should never feel uncomfortable because your language choices make you appear amateurish, the way I felt when a home improvement salesperson said to me, "Is my company the kind of company you want to do business with, and am I the kind of salesperson you want to buy from?" This salesperson left my home without a contract, unaware that I have a certain immunity to old-school closing tie-downs. I was embarrassed for him.

There is no reason to study unnatural, forced, or hokey language. You should never have to say things no one would ever say, or something that no one would ever feel comfortable saying when asking for a commitment.

You are a professional. You strive to be consultative, and to be your dream client's trusted advisor. The language you choose should reflect that level of professionalism. It should be natural, appropriate language, and it shouldn't make your client—or you—cringe when you open your mouth.

ALWAYS HAVE A BACKUP COMMITMENT

It isn't always easy to get the commitments you need. Sometimes a prospect will express fears and refuse to make the commitment you need to help them move forward in their buying process and your sales process. Oftentimes, there are backup commitments that, while not getting you everything you want, will get you a commitment that moves an opportunity forward.

For example, if you ask for information that isn't easy for your client to provide, a backup commitment might be to interview the people who can give you enough of that information to help you get the same outcome. A different backup commitment might be to ask to provide or sign a nondisclosure agreement so that your prospective client can be confident and comfortable providing you with the information you need.

Selling effectively requires that you be resourceful and creative. The backup commitment allows you to ask for something that moves an opportunity forward if and when your dream client refuses to make the commitment they really need to make. More important, the backup commitment protects you from damaging the relationship by arguing over a commitment that your prospective client isn't ready to make when there is another way available to you.

TIE COMMITMENTS TO WHAT IS COMPELLING THE CLIENT TO TAKE ACTION

You make it easier for your prospective client to say yes to your ask when you help them understand why you are asking for what you are asking for.

For example, if you need access to your dream client's operations team to build consensus around your solution, you will need to explain how gaining the support of other people on their team helps achieve the outcomes they want or need. "By bringing your operations team into this conversation now, we can make sure we dial in our solution so they get what they need and so we can get their support for changing your program. I want to make sure you get the improvement you need."

By tying the commitment to what is motivating your client to change, you provide them with a reason to say yes to the commitment you are asking for, instead of assuming they understand why the commitment is necessary and how they benefit. This also helps them understand the process of change and how they will eventually get the outcome they need.

The by-product of focusing on helping your prospective client with whatever is compelling them to change is that you eliminate the self-orientation that destroys your trust and credibility. You are asking them to commit to what is necessary to help *them* get what *they* want.

ASK!

Unless you haven't created enough value to earn the right to ask, there is no reason for you to be uncomfortable asking for the commitments you need to serve your prospective clients. Your prospective client knows you are a salesperson. They know you are eventually going to ask them to buy what you sell. They are not embarrassed or in any way disturbed by the fact that you are going to ask them to take next steps. You can't be either.

If you don't ask for the commitments you need, you are wasting your dream client's time, your company's time, and your own time. There is no reason to spend time in meetings only to leave with nothing resolved, nothing decided, and no next steps agreed upon.

The truth of the matter is, your dream client wants you to ask for their business. They want to work with someone who wants to help them solve their greatest and most pressing challenges.

In every sales interaction, you must ask for the commitment you need to serve your clients and to help them produce better outcomes.

ASK TO HELP NOW

It doesn't help to be slavishly devoted to your sales process, believing you can't possibly help your dream client until they complete all the steps your sales process requires. If your dream client has needs now, you need to ask for the opportunity to help, even if you haven't completed all the steps in your sales process.

If you recognize that your prospective client needs your help, and you have done enough to have earned the right to ask for their business, don't wait. Ask for their business, or ask for their orders. Start doing the work they need you to do. Otherwise, while you are taking your time going through your sales process, another salesperson may swoop in, ask for an order, and eliminate the need for your prospective client to have another meeting with you.

In one of my businesses, we ask for an order in every meeting. We do this as a matter of course. Even though we still continue doing the work necessary to understand their business and build the solution we will eventually provide, we also don't believe they should struggle if we can help them now.

Withholding your help isn't the right thing to do, even in a commercial relationship. You can begin working with your dream client, giving them the help they need, while you continue to do what your process requires of you.

DON'T MAKE YOUR CLIENT ASK YOU

We live in strange times. Some so-called sales experts suggest that there is never a reason to ask your prospective client to buy from you. Instead, you are supposed to wait passively until your prospect decides they want to take the next step. This advice is useless if your prospect doesn't even know what the next step should be.

Let me be crystal clear here: There is no scenario in which it makes sense for you to wait for your dream client to ask you if they can buy from you. Anyone who says otherwise is guilty of malpractice when it comes to offering advice on selling. You are not a better salesperson for not asking your client to take the next step or to buy from you. It doesn't make you more professional, nor does it make you less "salesy." If you believe that it does somehow make you less salesy, you should want to be more salesy.

Waiting for your prospect to ask you to take the next step makes you less consultative and less of a trusted advisor. Your client is counting on you to know what comes next and how they go from their current state to their future state. In fact, sometimes the best way to help your dream client is to ask for the commitment to get started and force them to make a decision they've been postponing because they are afraid to make the change they need to make.

Asking for the commitments you need to serve your dream client doesn't make you a bad or pushy salesperson. *Not* asking makes you a bad salesperson. It also makes you a time waster.

STOP TREATING CONCERNS AS OBJECTIONS

A long time ago, salespeople were taught to overcome objections. They were taught to explain in plain terms the logical reason their prospect should take action, and ask again.

If your dream client doesn't say yes to your ask, then they have some concern that you haven't yet resolved. If you don't resolve that concern, you are not going to get an affirmative answer by asking for the commitment you need over and over again.

An objection is the act of disapproving or disagreeing with something. The word "objection" isn't all that useful today. What is more useful is the idea of "resolving concerns." An objection is how someone informs you that they have a concern. Instead of focusing on the objection, you have to focus on resolving the concern.

The following are some of the real concerns your dream clients might have when they engage in the process of change; you need to treat them as such.

- If you don't understand what someone is trying to sell you, then you don't buy. You might say, "I don't want to move forward right now." That is the objection. Not really understanding what you are buying is the underlying concern that gave rise to that objection.
- If you don't believe that what someone wants you to buy is going to benefit you, you say no when they ask you to move forward. The

fact that you say no to a request to take the next step is an objection. The concern that is left unresolved is that you don't understand the value of making the purchase.

- If you are afraid of the risk that might be associated with a change you need to make once you buy, then you won't move forward until that risk is addressed—especially if the risk is personal, expensive, and potentially embarrassing.

If you leave your dream client's real concerns unaddressed, they are right to reject your request to take the next step or to buy whatever it is you sell. You have to ask to bring those concerns into the light so you can resolve them. That is your job as a consultative salesperson.

ALWAYS PROJECT CONFIDENCE

Always project confidence. If you've done good work in a sales interaction and created value for your prospective client, then you have earned the right to ask for the next commitment. If you have created value, asking for the commitment you and your client need to make together does not make you self-oriented, pushy, smarmy, manipulative, or "salesy."

If you are tentative or nervous about asking, you project a lack of confidence. That projected lack of confidence gives your prospect reason to believe that you haven't earned the commitment or that you don't believe the value proposition for that commitment. And if you don't believe that the commitment you are asking for is right and necessary, neither will your prospective client.

Confidence comes from knowing that you have the knowledge, skills, ability, and commitment necessary to produce some outcome. When you know what next steps are necessary and how they will benefit your client, you can confidently ask for the commitments you need. If you have the skill and ability to help your prospective client produce better results, asking for the next commitment is easy and natural.

As a very young man, I had a medical condition that caused me to need complicated brain surgery. I met with the best surgeon in the world when it came to performing this type of surgery, the removal of a large group of arteries and veins that had grown into a mass that was putting pressure on my brain. I asked questions; the surgeon answered calmly and slowly. He said as few words as possible and told me the truth, including the fact that he couldn't know what might happen after the surgery.

I asked the surgeon if he could successfully remove this mass of arteries and veins. He said yes. I asked him if he had done many of these surgeries before, and he said, "Thousands." At the time, I wished he was more conversational. But his confident demeanor made it easy to trust him. The last thing you want is a nervous, uncertain brain surgeon.

And the last thing your dream client wants is a nervous salesperson who lacks the confidence to ask for what he needs and who is unsure of himself.

Look, in many cases, if your prospective client could produce the results they want without making some of the commitments they need to make—including the Commitment to Change—they would already be producing those results. They wouldn't need you, and they wouldn't need what you sell. When you don't ask for those commitments, you are allowing them to continue to produce results that are less than they are capable of. This is how businesses fail. They don't do what is necessary and they don't make the changes they need to make. The result of this kind of failure is that people get hurt. They lose their company and people lose their jobs. Or they lose market share and fall behind.

Good salespeople are what prevents people and businesses from getting hurt. Poor salespeople avoid having difficult conversations and allow their prospective clients to continue doing what they are doing because they are uncomfortable having the necessary conversations and are afraid of asking for the commitments they need.

ALWAYS KNOW WHO HAS THE AUTHORITY TO SIGN

Decisions are now being made by consensus. The person on the prospective client's team with the responsibility for getting the outcomes you are selling may or may not have the authority to sign an agreement himself or herself. In a lot of cases, everyone on the buying committee has the power to veto a buying decision, and no one person can say yes all alone.

That said, there is still someone with the authority to sign a deal. You need to know who this person is because you will eventually need him or her to sign your contract. Even if this person is going to rely on the team to make the recommendation and would be unwilling to overrule them.

Even in a consensus sale, someone is "the authority."

FOCUS ON THESE GUIDELINES, NOT JUST THE WORDS

The words you use to ask for your dream client's business are less important than all the things you do leading up to that point.

This book is full of examples of language you can use to gain commitments. The words you use are important. Saying, "What's it going to take to get you to sign this contract"—words a salesperson actually said to me—is different from saying, "Can you share your concerns with me so I can make sure this works for you?" You can use the language in this book, and you can modify it to make it fit what and how you sell. These words are no replacement for a deep understanding of the underlying principles. Principles like: *Selling is not something you do to someone. It is something you do for someone and with someone.*

If you want to sell well, then first you need to be someone worth buying from. If you are struggling to gain commitments, review these guidelines and principles to see what you might change.

Chapter 15

TRANSFORMATIONAL CONVERSATIONS AND FEARING THE WRONG DANGERS

THERE ARE TWO MAJOR REASONS YOUR DREAM CLIENT REFUSES to make the commitment you ask them to make: The first reason is that they have some fear that prevents them from agreeing to move forward. The second is that they don't believe that making that commitment and taking the next step creates value for them.

In this chapter, we are going to look at what your dream client fears and why that fear causes them to avoid the commitment they need to make to move forward. If you want to serve your client and control the process, then you are going to have to identify, acknowledge, and address your prospect's fears.

FEAR OF WASTING TIME: DANGER OF NOT LEARNING ABOUT REAL CHALLENGES AND FUTURE OPPORTUNITIES

When your prospective client is concerned about your wasting their time, you resolve this concern by making the promise not to waste that time, and to trade something of value in exchange.

What it sounds like when your client has this concern:

- We are happy with our current partner.
- Can you call me back next quarter?
- Can you e-mail me information?
- Now is not a good time.

What it sounds like when you resolve this concern:

- I understand that you are happy with your current partner, and I promise to respect that relationship. I do still want to share with you these four big ideas, and I would like to know you. Should you ever need anything different, I hope I am the first one you think of. I promise I won't waste your time. It will be twenty minutes, and I'll leave you with some ideas and questions you will find valuable, even if we never work together.
- I know you get a lot of these calls, and it can be hard to tell who is worth your time and who isn't, and you can't meet with everyone. I promise you that I am not going to waste your time, and you will gain insights that can help you now and in the future. It will really be twenty minutes, and I promise—no pitch. I'll just share these ideas, and should you ever need me, you'll know how we think about these things.

In both of the examples above, you are trying to make it very clear that you understand the root cause of their concern: wasting time. Acknowledging these concerns and resolving them is what is necessary to gain the commitment of time.

FEAR OF DISCUSSING REAL ISSUES: DANGER OF UNADDRESSED ISSUES GETTING WORSE

If you want to be a trusted advisor, you have to help your clients resolve the root cause of their issues that prevent them from producing the results they need. Left unaddressed, these issues only grow worse over time.

What it sounds like:

- Everything is pretty good right now.
- Things aren't perfect, but we're currently doing fine.
- This is a problem, but it's just the way things are.

What it sounds like when you resolve this concern:

- I'm not sure if you are experiencing this, but a lot of people in your role are having trouble with [outcome], because the right way to do it used to be to [present the way your prospect is doing things]. Not a lot of people know that by changing the way this is done, they can eliminate that challenge from getting [that outcome]. Can I share that with you?
- We are seeing that companies that have started doing this differently are producing better results. I imagine you might have seen this, but can I show you our thoughts on how it might work for you?

In the above examples, I am assuming the prospective client doesn't want to get into their real issues, because they are concerned about being judged, about not knowing something, or about addressing the issue itself. In this case, you are trying to give the prospect air cover as a way to prevent them from having to protect their ego or fear.

FEAR OF CHANGE: DANGER OF OBSOLESCENCE (OR WORSE)

You will have prospective clients who fear change. They won't tell you that they are afraid of change. However, as you know, change shouldn't be their greatest fear.

What it sounds like when your client is concerned about change:

- I'm not sure we can do this right now.
- We're going to need time to think about this.
- Now isn't the right time.

What it sounds like when you resolve this concern:

- This may not be the right time to change. What I am concerned about here is that by not moving in this direction, you risk falling behind in this area, and it may be more difficult to make this change in the future. Can you share with me how you might move in this direction and what you would need to be able to do this?

FEAR OF INVITING OTHER STAKEHOLDERS: REAL DANGER OF "NO DECISION" AND CHALLENGES GROWING WORSE OVER TIME

This is a very common fear, and the resistance to this commitment can be great. This causes many salespeople to avoid the conversation, when selling well and effectively requires engagement.

What it sounds like when your client fears building consensus:

- I can make this decision myself.
- I don't want to bring anyone else into this conversation.
- I have the authority to make this decision.

What it sounds like when you resolve this concern:

- I understand that you are going to control this initiative. Can I share with you my experience? When we don't bring the people who are going to be impacted and involved, later on they tend to object to the change or drag their feet when the decision is made without them. Is there a way we could bring in some people who will support this, and make sure we get their buy-in?
- How could we bring in some of your counterparts who would be open to this kind of change to help us get buy-in across the organization?
- I am afraid that if we don't do this, the resistance will be too great to produce the results we are capable of. What do you think we might do about this?

You have to expose the greater danger here. Without doing so, bad things happen. The internal stakeholders who have been left out resist the change or actively work to kill the opportunity. Or what is sometimes worse, you win and then you can't execute.

By sharing the real danger, you bring awareness to the issue, and from there you can work to find a way to bring in other stakeholders.

FEAR OF SPENDING MORE MONEY AND NOT GETTING BETTER RESULTS: REAL DANGER IS UNDERINVESTING AND NOT GETTING BETTER RESULTS

People are always going to be concerned about money. They are going to be apprehensive about spending more than is necessary. They are also going to worry about being taken advantage of, unless your price is pretty much in line with the industry norms.

What it sounds like when your prospective client fears investing more and not generating better results:

- That is more than we are paying now.
- We've been promised better results before, and we've been disappointed.
- What if we spend the money and don't get the results?

What it sounds like when you resolve this concern:

- I understand this is more than you are used to investing. One of the reasons you aren't generating the results you need is that a lot of people in our space aren't making the necessary investment. This investment is what is necessary to ensure that we achieve your objectives here. Without this investment, you risk getting the same results that caused you to decide to change in the first place.
- This is the exact investment necessary to produce the results we've been building this solution for. Is it the investment you are worried about or are you concerned about the results? If it's the investment, we can relook at the results and change the investment. If it's the results you are worried about, we are 100 percent confident that this is the investment necessary to generate them.

If you want to do good work, you have to make sure the investment allows your team to have the resources to produce the results your clients need. The investment needs to provide them with the money necessary to produce those results. Anyone can have any result they want, provided they are willing to pay for those results.

FEAR OF SHARING CONCERNS: DANGER OF MAKING A POOR DECISION DUE TO THE LACK OF INFORMATION

You will find that many of your clients fear sharing their concerns. One of their biggest fears is having to make a decision to buy from you, from someone else, or at all. The reason they withdraw from the process is because they don't want to be sold, and by that I mean they don't want to be asked to decide.

What it sounds like when your prospective client fears sharing their concerns:

- We like this very much. We're going to talk it over, and we'll get back to you in a couple of weeks.
- If you can provide us with the proposal, we'll look it over and get back to you when we've made our decision.

What it sounds like when you resolve this concern:

- I know you are going to want to spend time reviewing all of this with your team to come up with the best decision. I would want to do that as well. What we have found is that your team is going to have questions and concerns, and that we can often address their questions or resolve their concerns if we know what they are. Can we meet with you at the conclusion of that meeting to provide additional information? You'll still have to decide together, but I want to make sure we serve you through this process, and that you are 100 percent confident with your decision, whatever it may be.
- I'd like to ask you for a chance to resolve any concerns and answer any questions you or your team may have at the conclusion of your meeting. In my experience, sometimes issues come up that weren't

surfaced in earlier conversations, and we can often address those concerns, if we know what they are. Can we have a chance to respond to any questions or concerns at the conclusion of that meeting?

You get to play. You do not get to automatically win. This is an area where it is easy to lose control—and easy to lose a deal. You have to do your best here, especially knowing that your prospective clients can often choose poorly at this stage, because they have an unaddressed concern.

FEAR OF DECIDING BECAUSE THE COMMITMENT REQUIRES DEALING WITH CHANGE: REAL DANGER IS NOT DECIDING AND CONTINUING WITH A STATUS QUO THAT NO LONGER SERVES

The fear of deciding is at epidemic proportions right now. One of the biggest reasons is that your prospective clients have dysfunctional buying processes, much of which are predicated on mistaking unanimity for consensus. Consensus doesn't require a unanimous decision. Your dream clients may also fear deciding at all, because they are worried about how difficult it will be to change.

What it sounds like when your prospective client fears deciding:

• Now is not a good time. We'll look at this again in a few months.
• We have decided not to do anything for the time being.

What it sounds like when you resolve this concern:

• I understand this is a significant change. I know you know that things aren't going to get better on their own. I wouldn't be giving you my best help if I didn't tell you that I believe you are going to lose time, and you are going to lose the better results you need right now if you do nothing. Can we discuss what it would take for you to be able to confidently make this decision, and can we start over if we need to?

• I am afraid that things are going to get worse over time, and I know you understand the need to change or we would not have done all this work. Where did we go wrong and what do we need to do to move forward? I believe we should go back and meet with your team members individually to address their concerns and make whatever changes necessary to get back on track.

If you've gained all of the commitments leading up to the Commitment to Decide, you shouldn't run into this very often, but there will be times when you can't easily get a decision. The right thing to do is to gain the commitment to go back and start again, most likely at the collaboration, consensus, or review stages of this process.

FEAR OF EXECUTING BECAUSE IT MEANS HAVING DIFFICULT CONVERSATIONS, INVESTING TIME AND ENERGY, AND MAKING REAL CHANGE

At some point, you are going to have a client who wants change badly, who signs your contract, and then doesn't do what is necessary on their end to produce the results they need. Even when you do your best to manage your client's expectations and gain their commitment to make changes on their side, you can end up with real trouble if the results aren't easily produced and people are under pressure.

What it sounds like when your prospective client fears deciding:

- We have a problem. This isn't working.
- This is what we were worried about. We are going to have to stop this and go back to what we were doing.
- I am going to need to cancel our contract.

What it sounds like when you resolve this concern:

- We expected to run into rough patches. We should have done a better job preparing you for this. We are both going to need to make a few adjustments, and some of this will be difficult. But we will produce the results. On our side, we are going to make the following changes. I am going to need your help to make the subsequent changes on your side.

You might also want to say:

- We've been down this road before. I can assure you that you will get through this, and it will be worth it. I will be on-site to work with you, and we will give you all of the resources you need to get through this rough patch. I'll help you get this same commitment from your team.

In *The Only Sales Guide You'll Ever Need*, I wrote about the importance of accountability. If you want to be the person your clients turn to when they need help with change, and if you want an absolute right to their next opportunity, you are going to have to deliver the outcomes you sold.

None of these conversations are necessarily easy, but they are what separate you from salespeople who fear having these conversations, and do not know that the real danger is that they are irrelevant.

Chapter 16

MANAGING COMMITMENTS

THIS IS A BOOK FOR SALESPEOPLE. LIKE MY PREVIOUS BOOK, *The Only Sales Guide You'll Ever Need*, I wrote it as a field guide for saleswomen and -men to use to create and win new opportunities. That said, sales managers also have an important role to play, and the ten commitments give you a powerful framework for managing and leading your team.

OUTCOMES AND ACTIVITIES

No one wants to be a micromanager, and even fewer people want to work for one. As a leader, however, you may need to manage at the micro level, ensuring that your team focuses on and produces the most important outcomes. Two of the most important outcomes you need your team to achieve are creating opportunities and winning opportunities. Neither is easy to achieve, or happens without a tremendous amount of focus and energy.

The creation of opportunities begins with gaining the Commitment for Time. There are two reasons why your team may be failing to gain this commitment and the resulting opportunities. First, they may not be doing enough prospecting. If this is the case, you must demand more activity, and you may have to examine their schedules to ensure that they are investing the necessary time and energy. The second possible cause of a lack of appointments is ineffective prospecting, which is a more difficult problem to correct. This requires teaching, training, coaching, and developing the salesperson. In either case, creating opportunities always comes before winning those opportunities, so gaining the Commitment for Time is a critical first step for you and your team.

Not wishing to offend your salespeople—especially the very good ones—you may hesitate to ask about prospecting activity and meetings set. You may tell yourself that you shouldn't have to be directive, that you don't care how your people get the outcomes. Adopting this attitude is an abdication of your responsibility. If your people are struggling with the Commitment for Time, failure is all but inevitable—and that failure sits squarely on your shoulders. Hiring salespeople, neglecting them, then firing and replacing them with new people whom you also neglect is not a good strategy for developing talent.

The best way to monitor the acquisition of new opportunities is via a pipeline review. This is not an opportunity review, where you examine a single deal. In a pipeline review, you ask each member of the sales team what new opportunities they have created. You also ask how many first appointments have been conducted and how many are scheduled for the coming week. If you don't like asking these questions, consider how uncomfortable you'll feel when you miss your quota because you're trying so hard to be nice. And remember: You're not just letting yourself down by failing to really lead your team; you're letting them down as well, because many of them could shine if you would take the time to polish them.

PUSHING OPPORTUNITIES BACKWARD

The ten commitments give you an enhanced level of specificity when it comes to managing your pipeline and forecasting deals. They give you greater insight and greater accuracy, because you can monitor their progress by seeing if deals are progressing along through the commitments. You can also see if a deal has "jumped ahead" without the salesperson getting the proper commitments; if that happens, you know that trouble lies ahead. Each commitment skipped increases your odds of losing the deal.

A lot of people meet with salespeople without making the Commitment to Change, but without this commitment, there is no opportunity. So during the early stages of an opportunity, ask, "Why is this prospect changing now? What's compelling them?" If your salesperson can't provide you with a powerful reason, you will have to help the salesperson create that powerful case for change, or they're just wasting time—their time and the prospect's time.

Keep asking your salespeople if they are gaining the necessary commitments to move the opportunity along. Ask them, for example, who from the prospect's company they are meeting with. Then ask yourself if these are the people required to provide the necessary collaboration. Your saleswoman may be focusing on the fact that she's meeting with someone from the C-suite who she believes can make the decision, but you know that you must first secure the Commitment to Collaborate, and then actually collaborate. Hand in hand with collaboration goes consensus, which must be built, or there is an excellent chance the opportunity will die—or be handed over to a competitor.

Salespeople often want to jump to the Commitment to Decide, or may shy away from it because they fear hearing no. It's your job as manager to keep your salespeople focused on working the commitments.

It's your job to keep them moving through the list, well prepared for each new step, and progressing with confidence.

We all want to see deals flying through and emerging out the other end of the pipeline. That means we've done a good job and will be rewarded. But if a salesperson skips over any of the necessary commitments, you must push that deal back to the point at which the very last commitment was secured. For example, if a salesperson tells you that he is presenting a solution without having collaborated and built consensus, you must insist that he go back and do that work first. And it won't always be the salesperson alone trying to move forward without the commitments they need. In many cases, impatient clients, or those who don't understand the importance of the steps, will ask the salesperson to skip ahead.

I urge you to conduct pipeline reviews, inspecting the deals through the lens of the ten commitments. And don't hesitate to push deals backward if necessary. Remember: Your goal is to make everyone succeed, and you do that by keeping the deals moving along at the proper pace, securing one commitment after another as you progress toward the final one.

IMPROVING DEAL STRATEGY

The ten commitments also allow you to improve your deal strategy. Too often, salespeople make too few sales calls on major opportunities. They make a single discovery call, believing that they've achieved everything they needed to in a single visit. When the contact they are calling on provides their view of their company's challenges, the salesperson gets a partial view of those challenges—and potentially an incorrect view. During that single visit, the salesperson might also have garnered the support of one single individual within the prospect's company. This is a weak strategy, and one you must not allow.

When you sell, you are trying to create a preference for you, your company, and your solution. Half measures and poor sales strategies and techniques will not create that preference.

In most cases, more discovery is better discovery. The more stakeholders that share their view of the problem, the more complete the picture. It's much like the old tale from India about the six blind men touching an elephant and describing what an elephant is like. One says the elephant is like a pillar; another says a tree branch. Still others suggest the elephant is like a hand fan, a wall, a pipe. Each of the blind men is giving his impression—and it is true, but partial.

The way to improve your deal strategy is to ensure that proper discovery work is done, that you are helping solve the right problem, and that you understand the root cause.

The Commitments to Collaborate and Build Consensus create value for your prospective clients. What is a better deal strategy than working with your dream client to make sure the solution you propose is exactly right and that it has their full support? How can the solution that your prospect helped to design be the wrong solution?

Truth be told, deals are not often won in boardrooms. They're won long before you present to the stakeholders in the boardroom. Show-horse salespeople stand up in the boardroom, present, and field difficult questions. Plow-horse salespeople do the work that ensures that they obtain the win long before getting to the boardroom, making their presentation a formality and the outcome a fait accompli.

Deal strategy can include all kinds of things. It can include how you intend to deal with your competitor's certain-to-be-lower price. It might include the solution you recommend and how you integrate it with their existing processes. The list here is endless, but if that list doesn't include creating a preference for you, your company, and your solution, it is weak strategy. The value that your salespeople create when they collaborate and build consensus is how you create that preference.

It is easier to win hearts and minds when you spend time with those people whose hearts and minds you are trying to win. Collaborating is proof positive that you are taking the needs of the stakeholders you are meeting with into account. Doing what is necessary to mitigate anything in your solution that might cause problems for some groups of stakeholders can help you gain their support.

Asking questions during opportunity reviews like, "What have we done to dial this in so it exactly fits this client's needs?" or "Who has been left out of this process?" give you an idea of how you are going to fare when it is time for the client to decide. Questions like, "Who is on the buying committee, and whose support do we have and who are we missing?" can give you a view as to how well your salesperson is doing creating a preference—and how likely they are to win. A lack of details here is a hint that you need to dig deeper.

You want to improve your deal strategy during every interaction with the sales force, and the ten commitments will give you a framework for toughening up your plan to win.

TESTING THE COMMITMENTS

Here are some questions you can ask your salespeople in order to make sure they have secured the appropriate commitments at the appropriate time. For each stage, if the answers you receive indicate that the salesperson has gained the commitment, tell her to move to the next. If not, insist that she go back and get the missing commitment.

For the Commitment for Time, ask: "Tell me about the new appointments you have scheduled for next week." Or: "What new meetings have you had over the last couple of weeks?" If you do not inspect this outcome, you will never be confident that you are creating the opportunities you need, nor will you know if one of your salespeople needs help.

For the Commitment to Explore, ask: "What kind of issues reso-nated with your prospective client?" Or: "What did you show them that grabbed their attention?" Without something worth exploring, change is going to be difficult, and opportunities rare. The role of the salesperson is now one of change agent, and you have to be certain they can create the case for change.

For the Commitment to Change, ask: "Why is this prospect compelled to change and what is driving that?" And: "What date do they think is the right date by which to execute this change?" If there is no commitment to change, it won't happen. These questions don't ensure that you win a deal, but they increase your confidence that change is likely.

For the Commitment to Collaborate, ask: "What adjustments or changes does the client need us to make for this to work for them?" Or: "What are we going to need to get some air cover and give them what they want here?" One way to think about this is that if no changes have been made, you may not have created a preference for your company and your solution.

For the Commitment to Build Consensus, ask: "Who is on the buying committee here?" And: "Who is opposed to this change and why?" And: "Whose support do we have, and who supports something different?" The larger the deal, the more important it is to have a plan to develop consensus.

For the Commitment to Invest, ask: "Is what we are proposing worth paying more for and why?" And: "Are they prepared to invest more to get these outcomes?" If there has been no discussion of pricing, you can expect to get pushback, and you will likely end up with a more difficult negotiation.

For the Commitment to Review, ask: "Are they 100 percent confident in this solution?" And: "Is this proposal and solution something they can say yes to?" And: "What would cause them to say no?" There is no reason to give a prospective client a proposal they can't accept. Make sure that your salesperson has the yes they need before they provide a proposal and pricing.

For the Commitment to Resolve Concerns, ask: "What are they concerned about?" And: "What are we going to have to provide them in the way of proof that will make them 100 percent confident moving forward with us?" Assume there are concerns. Deals are lost here when concerns are left unresolved.

For the Commitment to Decide, ask: "How are you going to ask for their business?" You will be surprised by what you hear when you ask this question. It is your job to make sure your team knows how to professionally ask for their prospect's business.

For the Commitment to Execute, ask: "What do we need to change to help our new client get the outcome we promised?" And: "What do they need to change on their side?" And: "What support do you need from me to help make sure these things happen?"

This last one is tricky. You are asking the salesperson questions that could indict your own company. That's good, because your goal is to make sure everyone succeeds, and sometimes that requires you to help your salesperson get what's needed from your organization. This is where you inspire your team by showing them that you are on their side and will go to bat for them.

DEVELOPING PROFESSIONAL SALESPEOPLE

The ten commitments can be used as a window into the mindsets and skill sets possessed by the various members of your sales force. We touched on this idea earlier in this chapter when we saw that failing to gain the Commitment for Time was evidence of either an activity problem (too little prospecting) or an effectiveness problem (trouble trading enough value to command the prospect's time). Let's take a deeper dive here.

Difficulty gaining the discovery phase commitments, including the Commitment to Explore and the Commitment to Change, indicates that the salesperson is struggling to create a compelling case for change and that they may lack the ability to have the necessary conversations to do so. This is often caused by a lack of business acumen, a lack of confidence, or simply an unfamiliarity with the necessary talk tracks (they need to hear what good sounds like). Knowing this allows you to develop salespeople's skills through training, having them ride along with more senior or more seasoned salespeople, and assigning them projects designed to improve their business acumen.

Moving ahead through the commitments, collaborating and building consensus are skills of a higher order. When you see salespeople struggling to shepherd prospective clients through the process of collaboration and failing to build consensus, you know that you have work to do. Experience is the best teacher in this situation. Salespeople in need of improvement should watch what more successful salespeople do so that they can mimic what they see. You may also provide them with language they can use during those meetings, such as, "What would you need to change for this to exactly fit your needs here?" You are also going to have to help your team manage stakeholders, especially those from whom it is going to be difficult to gain support.

The mindset and skill sets leading up to the Commitment to Decide are also of a higher level. Many salespeople avoid discussing price until the last moment, fearing that early disclosure will kill their opportunity. If that's the case, they need to develop the ability to justify the delta between your price and what your prospective client is already paying, or the delta between your price and your competitor's price. You can test your salespeople by asking them to role-play a scenario wherein their prospect says, "Your price is way higher than your competitor's." See how your salespeople respond, whether they are able to calmly and persuasively defend the need to pay more for you than they would for your competitor. If they can't do so, work with them until they can, with confidence.

There is an excellent chance that your sales force will not ask for the Commitment to Resolve Concerns. No one has ever told them that they should. That said, many salespeople are afraid to probe for concerns. But unresolved concerns can undo all the good work that has been done up to this point, which is why you must tell your people to ask for this commitment. It's your job as their leader to make sure they know what concerns they need to look for or elicit, as well as how to help their clients resolve those concerns to their satisfaction. For each deal, ask your people about the concerns their prospects have. If they reply, "None," ask them why. The answer is obvious: If they don't know of any concerns, it's because they haven't looked for them.

COMMITMENT, COMMITMENT, COMMITMENT

I've often heard sales leaders say that they want "closers," but that isn't really what they need.

What they need is a sales manager who can teach his or her team how to work through the ten commitments—and who insists that they do so. The sales manager who does that will have a team that closes plenty of deals.

Chapter 17
IN CLOSING

YOU WON'T FIND MANY PEOPLE WHO WILL TELL YOU THIS, BUT "who you are" matters far more than "what you do." Although you may think that your prospective client is only buying the value in your product, service, or solution, the truth is that you are the larger part of the value proposition. If you don't believe this is true, then I ask you to explore how the top salesperson in every company succeeds with the same product, same pricing, and same competitive challenges of the salespeople who don't produce the same results.

While much of what is written about sales is directed toward the "what" you do, the "who" that is doing the "what" is crucial. Unfortunately, most sales organizations want to believe that the "what" matters most, because scaling a business means hiring people you can train to sell. Companies focus their training and development on product knowledge and sales skills, when they train at all. Driven by the pressure for financial performance, most sales managers focus on forecasting and ensuring that deals are closed. They know they need to coach and develop their people, but they are asked to do more and more, with very little ever coming off their plate.

This is my second book, following on *The Only Sales Guide You'll*

Ever Need. Both books are as focused on how to develop yourself personally as professionally. This is crucial, because if you want to help your dream clients succeed, you must drop the idea that sales is something you "do" to someone else for your or your company's benefit. To be successful in today's selling environment, you must embrace the idea that selling is something you do *for* someone and *with* someone. You have to be someone they think of as being part of their team.

This means that no part of the sales process can be about you or what you need. It means you must move away from being self-oriented and become other-oriented, dedicated to creating tremendous value for your clients by solving their problems and becoming their trusted advisor. When you do so, you will also be rewarded, personally and professionally.

While there is plenty of skills-related content in both of my books, and while both will help you become a much better salesperson, they both begin with the underlying premise that you must improve yourself if you want better results. Leading and managing change are skills of a higher order.

COMMERCIAL RELATIONSHIPS MATTER

Technology is changing the way we do business. And if you think the changes we've seen over the last decade are incredible, if not also disconcerting, you haven't seen anything yet. We feel as if we've been sprinting to keep up with it all, but what lies ahead is going to make it seem as if we were standing still.

As technological development races ahead, entire industries are being destroyed and reimagined. Our culture is evolving with and because of this technology. The very nature of our work and jobs is irrevocably changing beyond anything one might have imagined a few short decades ago.

One of the key changes in business is that technological advances have made it possible to transact faster and with less friction than ever. Much of what can be automated is being automated. Because we *can* transact, some people and some companies believe they *must* transact. As a result, there is a strong push toward the idea that commercial relationships are no longer going to matter. Many pundits and prognosticators predict that salespeople will soon be unnecessary, a relic of the past banished to the dust heap of history.

There are a few of us in the wilderness eating honey and locusts, warning those who are open to listening that there is another path—for those who would dare to take it. I say this because, even though technology has dramatically altered our lives over the past decade, century, millennium, and more, we have yet to see any change that has eliminated commerce between human beings. That isn't going to go away anytime soon.

Since the beginning of time, people with leadership responsibilities have surrounded themselves with trusted advisors, counselors who could help them make decisions and guide them to the future. No great leaders made decisions without counsel. It's certainly true that, at one level, technology will continue to change commercial relationships, and transactional purchases where no value can be created are going to become ever more transactional. At the same time, however, the larger, more strategic decisions are going to become more strategic still.

You have a place in that strategic future. But taking your place means that you are going to have to get better at getting better. Again, "who you are" matters more than "what you do," especially when it comes to change.

SELLING IS A CHANGE INITIATIVE

The skills of sales have gone through three major periods. As soon as people started trading, they needed to know how to prospect, present, and close. These are first-generation skills, and they are still completely necessary. As we moved into the industrial age, new skills were required, like differentiating your offering, diagnosing your client's needs, and negotiating. These second-generation skills are also still necessary, but insufficient by themselves. In this third generation, a post–industrial age, new skills are required. These include business acumen, change management, and leadership, because in large, complex, business-to-business sales, it's not enough to offer a client a good product or service and then walk away. Many times, you are asking that they change their way of doing something, and change is always difficult. It's difficult to embrace the idea of change, it's difficult to agree to change, it's difficult to begin initiating and then to adapt to that change, and it can be difficult to sustain the change.

This makes you an agent of change, a catalyst, instigator, agitator: a change manager. You are selling your dream client a better future that requires them to break from the past, let go of what they know, and step into the unknown. And it requires you to walk alongside the client, always focused on their success. This book has described that path in detail, and it's what you must be prepared to do. It's literally how you create compelling, differentiated value. If your clients could produce the results they are capable of without you, they would already be doing so. If your competitors could help them, they wouldn't need you.

YOU SELL AS A PEER

Your prospective clients don't want a subservient, fearful salesperson who avoids dealing with difficult issues. They no longer need someone who can share with them only the features and benefits of a product or solution, someone who lacks the depth to have a business conversation. Your prospective clients' needs have radically changed over the last two decades. In some ways, selling hasn't kept pace. Sales organizations haven't prepared salespeople to become their dream clients' peer. They haven't focused on building a whole business person, someone with the depth and knowledge to serve their clients.

It isn't enough to know how your solutions solve your clients' problems. That's table stakes. You are now required to recognize problems your client doesn't yet recognize. You must also be able to explain where your client has better results available to them, even before they recognize that this is true. A good salesperson now sounds like a good general manager, and someone who could work in their client's company. They have a greater depth, gravitas.

To be a peer, you have to be able to make the case for change. You must be able to instigate that change. This isn't something a salesperson has traditionally had to do. It used to be enough to provide the right solution when your dream client recognized that they had a problem. Now you have to be the one to recognize the problem, build the case for change, and provide the solution.

Being a peer means that you make and defend the case for change. It also means that you know how to lead that change, helping your client transform what they are doing and generate better results. A peer doesn't avoid the difficult conversations required to bring change. Nor does a peer allow their client to avoid doing what is necessary to generate better results. You have to have transformational conversations, and you have to be capable of helping people come to a consensus about what must be done, even when some disagree and even when some oppose that change.

A trusted advisor doesn't wait until their client suffers the consequences of continuing down a path that no longer serves them. A trusted advisor uses their trust and influence to have difficult conversations, and they use their advice to help their clients choose a different path. If you have ever said that you want to be a trusted advisor or consultative salesperson, this is what you have signed on for.

IN CLOSING

There are countless great books on different aspects of sales. They focus on a single topic, like prospecting, negotiating, presenting, or some other skill. They are all useful. But because the role of sales has changed—and continues to change—you are going to see more books that focus on the higher-level skills, such as becoming a change manager and learning to look at the process of selling through the lens of the commitments required to assist your clients through the buyer's journey. This is one of those books.

The commitments you studied in this book are those required to help your dream clients change and produce better outcomes. The very best salespeople today—those who will continue to be in demand in the future—are those who know how to create a compelling case for change and lead their clients through that process. This is going to matter more and more as we move into a future of accelerating disruptive change.

Use this book to create and win new opportunities. Use it to help your clients produce the better outcomes they need, and that they can accomplish through your help as a change agent and trusted advisor. Apply the principles and ideas in this book to help the people you care about make changes in their lives. What you do makes a difference.

If you want to keep pace with these ideas and the changes in sales, I invite you to read my blog (www.thesalesblog.com) and join my Sunday Newsletter (www.thesalesblog.com/newsletter), where you will continue to learn about human relationships, growth, and change. You can also find my daily vlog at www.youtube.com/iannarino.

Connect with me on Twitter (@iannarino), Facebook (www.face book.com/thesalesblog), and LinkedIn (www.linkedin.com/in/ianna rino). Send me an e-mail at anthony@iannarino.com and share your success stories.

And come visit me at www.thelostartofclosing.com for worksheets, workbooks, and additional resources.

Now go and do good work!

WITH GRATITUDE

At the time this book is published, it will be less than ten months from the publication of *The Only Sales Guide You'll Ever Need*. The list here hasn't changed much, but my gratitude has grown immeasurably.

I am ever grateful for my wife and best friend, Cher Iannarino. There is no way you knew what you were signing on to when we started this adventure, and I thank you for your support, which has always been unconditional and unwavering.

Aidan, you are mature beyond your years, and you have the highest level of consciousness of any person your age that I have ever known. I am thankful for the man you are becoming, and the knowledge that you will exceed me.

Mia, you are beautiful on the outside, and even more beautiful on the inside. I am grateful for your sense of justice, and the fact that you are more powerful than you know.

Ava, you are the strongest-willed and most determined person I have ever met. I am grateful for your indomitable spirit, and I am thankful for who you will become when you channel your passion.

Mom, there are no words to convey my gratitude for who you are, for what you have made me, and for the sacrifices you have made for all of your children, as well as the people who you have treated as if they were your own. Your example of character has shaped me more than anything else.

Dad, for your constant belief in me, and for giving me two books that I should not have read at thirteen years old.

Thada Larimer, Tara Iannarino, Jason Iannarino, and Mike Iannarino. If I could have chosen my brothers and sisters, I would have chosen you.

Peg Mativi, Geoff Fullen, Brandy Thompson, Matt Woodland, Becky Kukay, Ron Zinko, Kelly Stinedurf, and the rest of my family at Solutions Staffing and IFG.

Adrian Zackheim, Will Weisser, Kaushik Viswanath, Alyssa Adler, and Katherine Valentino at Portfolio Penguin Random House, for your belief in my work and your help with both of my books. Beth Mastre, Heather May, Amy Tobin, Francesco Lazzarro, Damian Wohrer, David Gardner, Amber Herth, Bob Cabcaras, Zach Hoover, Barry Fox, and Carey Green.

You are born with some brothers, and others you choose. Mine include Jeb Blount, Mark Hunter, and Mike Weinberg. I appreciate your friendship, and our little thing.

Nathan Speiser, Patrick Gallagher, Jim Bostick, David Lawrence, Steve Malvesta, Jeff Smith, Britney Francis, Steve Byrne, Terri Kachinsky, Sarah Kilburg, Christina Ritchie, Bryan Thomas, Brian Yarmowich, Bill Proctor, Ricky Arriola, Jason Schlenker, Dan Arriola, Christina Canizares, John Watkins, Jay Herther, John LaBrosse, Mike Sheridan, Wayne Deceasare, Sarah Curtis, Doug Rutherford, Reagan Evans, Rob Magness, Judy Toland, Troy Florance, Dan Kirwan, Matt Bintliff, Shannon Davis, Patrick Farramond, Jimi Marshall, Matt Steele, Casey Bobb-Etter, Darren Alcock, John Pecaric, Jodie Boedlt, Jim Marks, Larry Klein, and Steve Finzer.

Lahat Tzvi, Miles Austin, John Spence, Mike Kunkle, Leann Hoagland Smith, Matt Heinz, Lori Richardson, Doug Rice, Paul McCord, Tibor Shanto, Alen Mayer, Bob Terson, Karin Bellantoni, Kelley Robertson, Todd Schnick, Alice R. Heiman, Gary Hart, Nancy Nardin, Andy Paul, Steven Rosen, Elinor Stutz, Richard Ruff and Janet Spirer, Dianna Gearin, Deb Calvert, Jack Malcolm, Jeff Beals, Jim Keenan, Babbette Ten Haken, Dan Waldschmidt, Tim Ohai, Kelly Riggs, Dorian Lynn Hidy, Doyle Slayton, Lee Bartlett, and Kelly McCormick.

Douglas Burdette, Michael Flynn, Donald Kelly, Phil Gerbyshak, Dave Savage, Anthony Conklin, James Carbary, Will Barron, and Paul Watts.

Dave Brock, Gerhard Gschwandtner, Bob Burg, Michael Port, Bruce Turkel, and Lolly Daskal.

Ken Wilber, for providing me new eyes through which to view the world.

INDEX